POPULAR NETCRAFT

By

H. T. LUDGATE

"I personally commend this fine book to every sportsman who enjoys making things. The pleasure and satisfaction derived from making your own equipment as shown here will repay you well for your trouble in working out the details. This is by far the finest book available on net making."

FRANK R. STEEL

Editor of The Fishing Tackle Digest;

Author of numerous books on fishing;

Staff writer for the leading sportsmen's magazines.

Published By

NETCRAFT COMPANY

"Hard To Find Specialties For Fishermen"

3101 Sylvania Avenue

TOLEDO 13, OHIO

NETCRAFT COMPANY
Toledo 13, Ohio
7th Edition

ACKNOWLEDGMENTS

TO MY fishermen friends all over the world whose keen interest in net making has been a source of inspiration, I am deeply indebted. Your kindly criticism and frequent suggestions have made this present manual possible.

The following specific contributions I acknowledge with sincere gratitude:

Atlantic Fisherman. Illustrations and detail on mending Nets.
Bibb Manufacturing Co., Macon, Ga. Hints on handling twine.
Chicago Natural History Museum—Illustration from exhibit of Swiss Lake Dwellers.

R. J. Ederer Co., Chicago. Illustrations and detail on commercial fishing nets.

O. A. Friemoth — For details on his pipe frame for turtle trapping.

Fishing Gazette, New York. Illustrations and detail on commercial fishing methods.

Mr. Lester Griswold. For material reprinted from his popular book: "Handicraft — Simplified Procedure and Projects." Outwest Bldg., Colorado Springs, Colo.

Otto Wilhelm — My Alabama friend whose sparling letters, sketches, and enlightening notes have aided materially in these net making instructions.

Mr. Clyde Weirick. Pictures of his turtles and hints for trapping.
Finally, my special acknowledgment and thanks to Dave Robeson, sportsman and friend, whose illustrations throughout this manual have unveiled the secrets of net making.

H. T. LUDGATE
Walloon Lake, Michigan

CONTENTS

WELCOME

Ahoy! My friend, Aboard, Aboard,
And shipmates we shall be
   Where the salt spray whips
   And the white cap dips
Far out on a fishing sea.
We'll make our nets, like salty vets
Each knot of twine made fast
   And row upon row
   We'll watch it grow
A thing of beauty, a thing to last.

Swiss Lake Dwellers — 3,000 Years Ago
Courtesy Chicago National History Museum

ROMANCE OF NET MAKING

An Ancient Art Is Reborn!

ONE OF the oldest crafts known to man is that of making nets. Of course no one knows for sure when the first nets were made but without doubt it goes back to earliest prehistoric times. The Swiss Lake Dweller's scene from an exhibit at the Chicago Natural History Museum (Field Museum) would date the making of nets at least 3,000 years ago and even then the art seems to have been pretty well developed. There isn't a country in all the vast expanses of the globe wherein net making has not played an important part. The livelihood of countless

millions has been enmeshed in the simple net—down through the ages
in myriads of coastal villages and out of the way places the fisherman has
deftly tied the priceless netting knot. From father to son, or neighbor to
neighbor, the knowledge was passed, but with the coming of machine made
nets the secrets were kept by a relatively few "Old Salts" who were char-
acteristically close-mouthed about their skill.

The romance, therefore, of this unique craft is stirring to our imagina-
tion today. Like the primitive urge to hunt which has left its inherent
stamp on mankind, the primitive art of net making stirs something within
us akin to primitive self preservation—the earliest and strongest driving
motive in man or beast. When a man couldn't eat unless he caught it,
his greatness and stature in his little community relied solely upon his
hunting and fishing skill, a grim, earnest business with life in the balance.

Is it any wonder then that amidst all the comforts and overstuffed
luxuries of today that we glean a bit of elemental refreshment as we take
up net making as a hobby? We, too, can let ourselves go back to the primitive man within us and revel in the skill of our hands. Without thought
of time or hourly return, the rhythm of making knot after knot furnishes
relaxation and simple enjoyment that is priceless in our tense moving
world. To those who don't understand the motive that drives us to
hunting and fishing haunts in all kinds of weather, net making will seem
an impractical waste of time. It's like a well meaning tackle dealer (he
should have been selling groceries) who couldn't understand why a person
should make a net when he could sell 'em one so cheaply. It would have
been useless to explain to him that upon returning from a swell fishing
trip on which we have spent plenty of "dough" in tackle and expenses,
that we don't compare the cost per pound of our catch with that offered at
the fish market. Useless, too, to explain that we go back again, and again,
each time with increasing enjoyment. No, net making is not a hobby to
explain,—it is one simply to enjoy.

In the years since NETCRAFT was founded (1941) the extent of the
interest in this craft has been amazing. People from every walk of professional, business and workingman's life have become interested. Doctors
and professional men by the hundreds, heads of businesses large and small,
high ranking officers, home sick GIs, veterans in hospitals all over the

land, trappers in snow bound cabins, forest rangers on their lonely out-posts, old-time settlers in Alaska, turtle trapping villagers in the deep south, and subway riders of Manhattan—from every station the common urge which binds us as "outdoorsmen" has found a common and inex-pensive outlet in net making. Included in this odd family are the editor of a large metropolitan daily, an executive of a big steel plant, a famous movie star and countless smaller lights and "glimmers." Letters by the score are on file expressing the pleasure and satisfaction that net making has given. With all due respect to the upper crust who have found pleasure in net making, this material however is written primarily for plain old civilian "Joe," the guy of moderate or little means who takes his fishin' fun as he can find it,—maybe night crawlers today and flies tomor-row, if bass aren't hittin' then catfish will do, gets all hepped up over turtle trappin'; in fact, name your mud bank, pond, lake or open stream

Making Fish Nets, Lake Chapala, Jalisco, Mexico
Photo by E. A. Goldman, Fish and Wild Life Service

that doesn't find him interested in what you might catch there and how you might catch it. There is the man after our own heart and, as brothers under the skin, our search in his behalf will never cease for new and unique methods as well as rare and forgotten fishing devices.

Making fish nets is often a family affair. This is true in Mexico as shown in the picture here of Net Making on Lake Chapala, and it is equally true here in the United States. In a small Down East town, a mother writes of the curiosity and amazement her family scene arouses with each one doing his "Nettin',"—grandfather working on a landing net, mother and daughter on shopping bags or snoods, and father and son doing a set of turtle traps.

Women have a natural fondness for net making and are well represented among the ardent followers of this unique craft. The romance of net making has also appealed to youngsters. They pick up the knot detail from the pictures and readily turn their new skill to good account.

Drying the Nets At Gloucester, Mass.

HOW TO MAKE A REAL LANDING NET
PLENTY DEEP AND PLENTY STRONG

Recommended As An Ideal Starter To Learn Basic Details
of Net Making.

THE VALUE of making your own landing net is that you can make it RIGHT. You can put the right stuff in it—high grade American, long staple cotton, and every knot pulled up right so as to last. What's more you can make the net plenty wide and plenty deep. With a little pains you can turn out a piece of equipment that will give you years of satisfactory service and plenty of fun in the making.

The essential tools for net making are as follows: (See Page 12.)

1. A shuttle to hold the twine. Fig. 1.
2. A gage stick which keeps the meshes uniform and determines their size. Fig. 2.
3. A stiff, round stick or metal rod on which the work is all done in the flat. Fig. 10.
4. Seine Twine. No. 12 Medium is a good size for landing net (less than a quarter pound required).

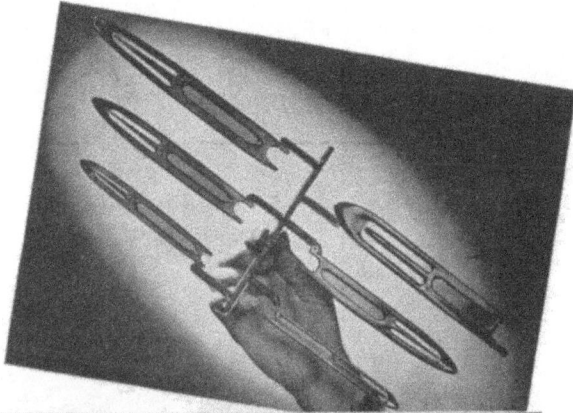

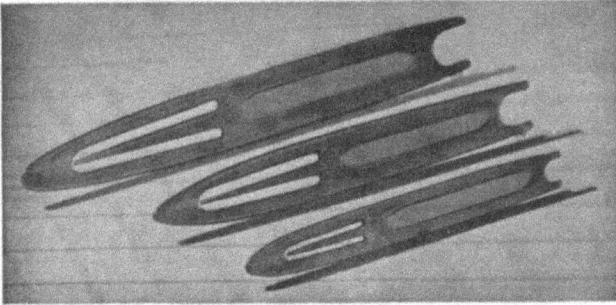

Shuttles were formerly carved out of wood by the Oldtimers. However, our modern plastics give us a shuttle that is far superior. Our NETCRAFT, patented shuttles afford maximum flexibility so necessary in rapid winding; they are also light in weight and waterproof.

Here is a complete range of shuttle sizes for small and large work.

Description	Width	Length
Netcraft Small Shuttle	$\frac{3}{4}''$	$5\frac{1}{4}''$
Netcraft Narrow Shuttle	$\frac{1}{2}''$	$5\frac{1}{2}''$
Netcraft Medium Shuttle	$\frac{7}{8}''$	$6\frac{1}{4}''$
Netcraft Large Shuttle	$1''$	$7\frac{3}{4}''$
Netcraft Wide Shuttle	$1\frac{1}{8}''$	$7\frac{1}{2}''$
Netcraft Jumbo Shuttle	$1\frac{1}{8}''$	$10\frac{1}{2}''$

The rod can be a maple dowel stick, about ⅜" diameter or larger, available at any hardware store, or if you can find a solid metal rod, such as is sometimes used in drying curtains, that is fine too. The rod may be supported by a pair of screw eyes driven into the edge of a bench or table. The support should be solid because a continual pull will be exerted each time a knot is pulled tightly.

If you are going to work in a living room, or any place where nails and screws cannot be driven, then tie two loops of string at the back of a heavy piece of furniture and simply slip the rod into the string loops, one for each end.

FILLING THE SHUTTLE.   The shuttle is filled by winding the twine around the tongue of the shuttle, then down around the heel and up on the other side where it goes around the tongue again and back down. In other words, you describe a series of "U"s. Turn the shuttle over each time you go around the heel. Those who are in the business bend the nose or end of the shuttle downword each time they wrap aroung the tongue. They use the thumb of the same hand that holds the shuttle. By bending the nose downward you leave the tongue point exposed. If you find this unhandy, then expose the tongue point simply by pushing it outward each time you wind. Notice that the shuttle will not unwind by itself if accidentally dropped.

Start by using the medium size shuttle. It is best for all-round work. Later you may want to own, as many net makers do, a complete set of shuttles so as to be able to choose a size shuttle best suited for the work undertaken.

For example, the landing net here described can be made satisfactorily with the medium size Netcraft Shuttle, however, the large size shuttle with this size mesh (2¾" stretched measure) works better as it holds more twine and leaves fewer tied places in this finished job.

HOW TO USE TWINE FROM A SKEIN.   Stretch the skein between two spikes driven into a bench or piece of plank,—see left side of lower picture on page 16. Only when thus stretched out should the ends be untied. Untie both ends and whichever end unwinds the easiest is the outside end from which you will load your shuttle. Leave twine between spikes until all used.

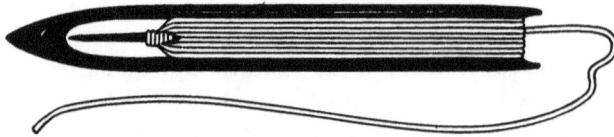

1 MEDIUM SHUTTLE
*WIND TWINE ON SHUTTLE
UNTIL FULL.
HOLDS 5 TO 10 YARDS*

WRAP TWICE AROUND
GAGE STICK, TIE TIGHT,
TIE AGAIN, THEN SLIP
LOOP OFF AND HANG
ON NAIL

NOTICE POSITION
OF FIRST KNOT

GAGE STICK

2

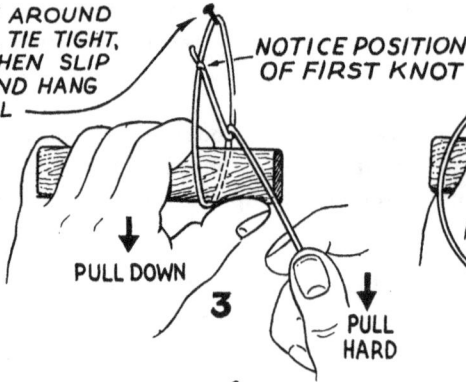

PULL DOWN

3

PULL HARD

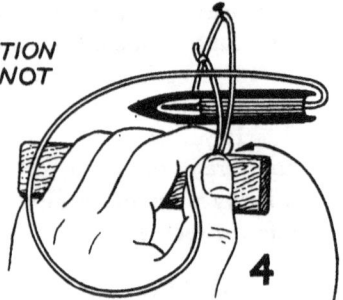

4

PINCH & HOLD TIGHT
WHILE KNOT IS
BEING TIED

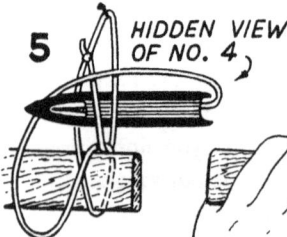

5 HIDDEN VIEW
OF NO. 4

6 LEFT THUMB & FORE-
FINGER MUST CONTINUE
PINCHING WHILE KNOT
IS TIGHTENING

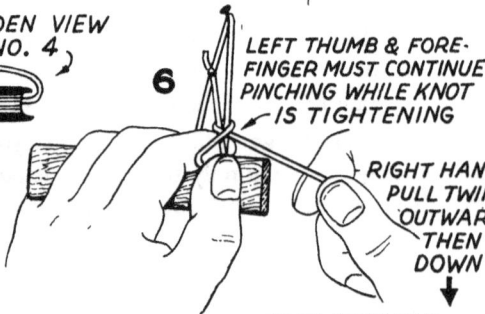

RIGHT HAND...
PULL TWINE
OUTWARD
THEN
DOWN

7 **8**

RIGHT   WRONG

IMPORTANT!

*WHILE TIGHTENING,
DON'T LET KNOT
SLIP BELOW "V"*

HOOK, BENT NAIL
OR TWINE LOOP

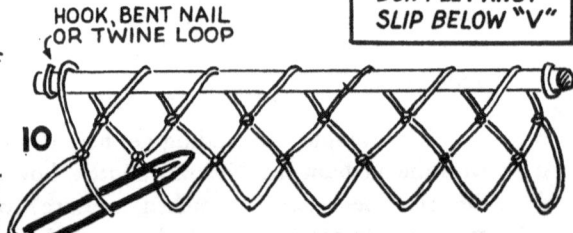

10

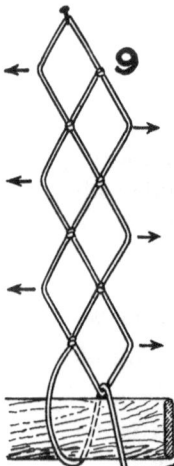

9

MAKE A CHAIN OF
STARTING MESHES
BY TYING KNOTS AS
IN NO. 4. AFTER
EACH KNOT IS TIED
PULL OUT THE GAGE
STICK AND TIE AN-
OTHER AS SHOWN
HERE.
STRAIGHTEN OUT
MESHES BY PULLING
WITH FINGERS AS
SHOWN BY ARROWS

THREAD THE STARTING MESHES ON A
STIFF ROD AS SHOWN ABOVE...THEN
BEGIN NEXT ROW AS SHOWN IN
FIGURE II. PINCH AT "B" AND
TIE EXACTLY AS SHOWN IN
FIGS. 4, 5 & 6. KEEP TWINE
TIGHT ON GAGE STICK. THE NEWLY MADE MESHES
SHOULD BE LEFT ON GAGE
STICK UNTIL CROWDED,
THEN SLIP OFF SOME. AT END
OF ROW, PULL GAGE STICK
OUT, TURN ROD END FOR
END AND START OVER...
PULL KNOTS TIGHT!

11

PULL

PULL

B

PULL DOWN

© 1945 NETCRAFT

ROBES

FIRST A CHAIN OF MESHES. To begin you first make a chain of meshes in the manner shown in Figs. 4 through 9. Do not attempt a net right away but simply do a dozen starting meshes (these will be in the form of a chain). The starting meshes can then be transferred to the rod and a few rows of regular meshes added for practice.

A word about this starting chain. It is nothing more than duplicating, one beneath the other, the knot which is started in Fig. 5. Each time, of course, you have to remove the gauge stick to drop down in position to make the next knot. If you have a long starting chain you'll find it handy to rehang the chain on one of the lower links every half dozen meshes or so to avoid too long and stretchy an affair to handle.

Once you master the starting meshes you are over the "hump" and the rest is really fun, for you leave the gauge stick in place and can go right along making mesh after mesh easily and as uniform as chicken wire.

TRANSFERRING STARTING MESHES TO ROD. Straighten out the starting meshes by pulling with fingers as shown in Fig. 9. Slip the first row of starting meshes onto the rod as shown in Fig. 10. The shuttle end should be on the left and you will now work from left to right. When you get to the end of a row you will simply lift your rod up off its hooks and turn it end for end. You have probably been wondering what to do when you come to the end of the twine that you wound on the shuttle. Simply refill the shuttle from your ball or skein and tie onto the old work with a square knot. This extra knot will give you no trouble. Notice that when you start the netting on the rod, Fig. 11, you do not remove the meshes from the mesh stick. Leave them on as it will keep your work even. When the stick gets crowded, slip off a few meshes. With practice you will soon learn the netting knot and speed and uniform meshes will follow. You will find it helpful to learn not to let go of the shuttle but to pass it through each successive loop by holding it between the little finger and one next to it, then after it is passed through the loop grip it with the thumb and forefinger. Make this pass entirely one handed.

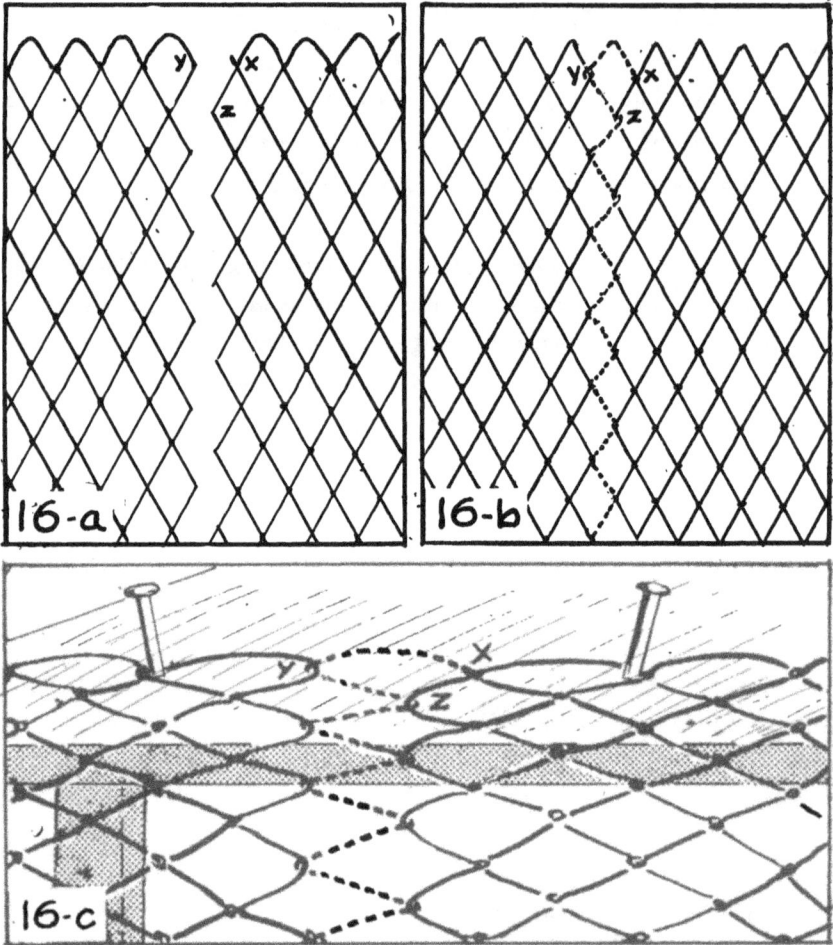

16-a

16-b

16-c

HOW TO CLOSE OR SEAM A NET

THIS OPERATION is necessary for all work that is done in the flat which must be converted into a tube or cylinder or cone shape, such as landing nets, live bags, shopping bags, etc. Obviously, if the work is done on a Netcraft Wheel this seaming operation is eliminated.

Study pictures 16-a and 16-b to see just what takes place. Notice the shape and position of the facing edges and notice how the closing string—the dotted line, starts at X then ties at Y, then Z, etc. Do not use a gage in this operation but judge the distances with your eye. If the work is done right you really can't tell where the closing of the net took place.

To do this fancy trick of closing, drive two nails about seven to eight inches (three stretched meshes) apart and hang the netting as shown. All the left hand knots are tied overhand as shown on page 23, passing the shuttle from the top downward. All the right hand knots are tied with the shuttle coming up from the bottom in the usual manner. Rehang the netting on the nails as you go along so that you'll always have a direct pull to keep the diamond shape of each mesh uniform. You'll find it helpful to shift your body—first facing toward the left nail while tying at Y, then facing toward the right nail when tying as at Z. This closing of a net is a valuable skill to learn and we recommend that you persevere until you have it licked.

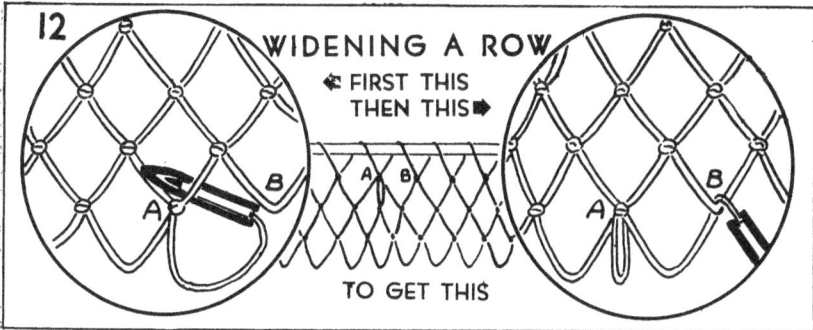

WIDENING A ROW
◀ FIRST THIS
THEN THIS ▶
TO GET THIS

HOW TO WIDEN NETTING
(Increasing Netting)

This trick enables you to increase the number of meshes in a row. Instead of knitting from "A" to "B" as you ordinarily would, make a second loop through "A" and tie the netting knot, then proceed to "B." This extra loop you have created is to be treated the same as any other loop in making the next row of mesh beneath it.

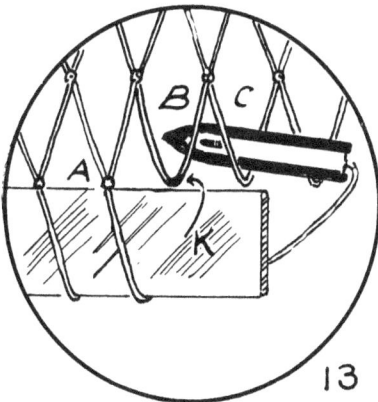

HOW TO NARROW NETTING
(Decreasing Meshes)

Refer to illustration No. 13. Instead of going from "A" through just loop "B" as you ordinarily would, pass the shuttle through two loops ("B" and "C") and tie the regular netting knot as usual. Thus you have eliminated one mesh.

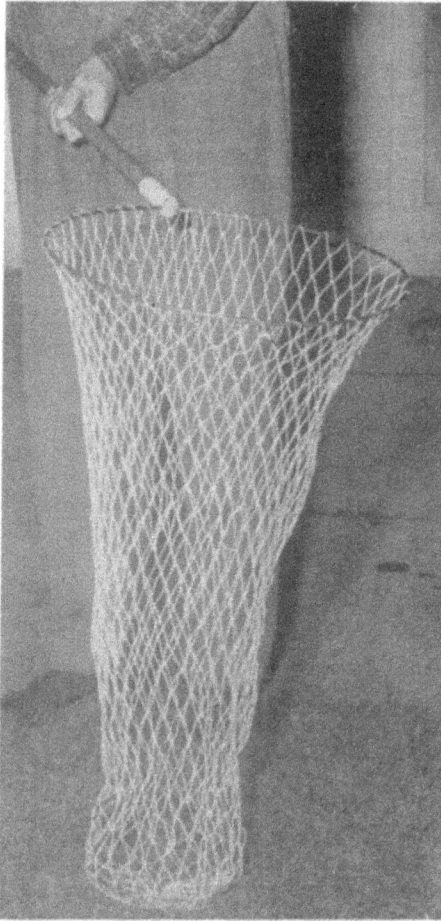

Row Upon Row You Watch It Grow

HERE you see the landing net being made in the flat. The meshes come off the gage stick all the same size—orderly and uniform. Constant tension of the left hand against the gage stick and firm pulling up of the knots makes for fine workmanship. Notice the method of holding a skein of twine between two spikes.

The finished net shown here is plenty deep and wide—it's a pleasure to use. Equipment like this gives added pleasure to your fishing and is comfortable insurance against bad breaks in difficult landings.

HERE ARE COMPLETE DETAILS FOR YOUR CUSTOM BUILT LANDING NET

NOW WITH the foregoing as preliminary practice you are ready to make your first netting project which we suggest be a landing net with a 16" mouth opening.

Use the medium gage stick (approximately 1¼" wide), and a medium shutle,—the ones that come with the Netcraft kit. Use No. 12 twine.

Make a chain of 39 starting meshes. This is done by tying 78 knots one beneath the other as shown in Fig. 9, page 12. This chain of knots, before slipping onto the rod will be over nine feet long.

Lay this starting chain out flat and open it up with your fingers as shown by the arrows in Fig. 9. Now loop the top row of mesh on to your holding rod as shown in Fig. 10. DON'T GET THIS STARTING CHAIN UPSIDE DOWN.

After each row turn the stick over and start a new row, always working from left to right. Make eight rows of knots, each row being full 39 knots to the row. In the ninth row and once in every row thereafter do the narrowing stunt as shown in Fig. 13, page 15. This reduction of two meshes into one can be done anywhere in the row but in the successive rows stagger the position so the heavier knots do not all come beneath each other.

When you slip the net off the holding rod in preparation for bringing the sides together you will find that the whole business when stretched tight and bunched like a rope measures 38 inches in length. This is mentioned to give you some idea that you are coming along about right and have followed directions well.

CLOSING THE NET.   In general, the landing net is completed by closing the sides together to form a sleeve like affair, or tube. Then this open bottom, conical shaped tube is closed at the bottom by a bone ring. Follow the instructions on Page 14 for closing the net. Give this your careful attention for it is about the most difficult operation in netting.

Note: If many nets are to be made where speed and uniformity are important we suggest the Netcraft Wheel—see page 30. It eliminates the tedious seaming operation.

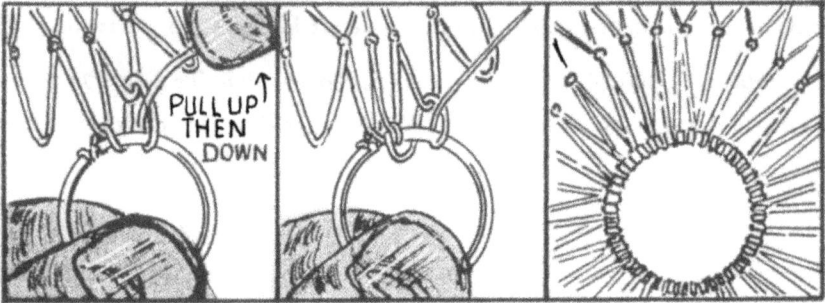

How To Close the Bottom of a Net

A ¾-inch bone ring makes a neat finish for a landing net, live bag or shopping bag. The pictures show the method. Do not use a shuttle but simply cut off a piece of twine a foot or so long and use your fingers to make the passes through the loops. It will help to double the string when pushing it through. You'll notice that the string passes DOWN through the ring before picking up the next mesh. On a net made of No. 12 medium twine and also using the same size twine for the tie string you can jam in as many as 20 to 23 meshes on a ¾-inch bone ring.

LOOK WHAT YOU'VE GOT.   The finished net when hung on the wire frame, as in the picture on page 16, will be about 33 inches deep. This is much deeper than the store net you see, but in actual use in safely handling big fish, you'll never go back to a shallow net once you have used a deep net. The net part alone, if made from No. 12 seine twine according to directions, will weigh around three ounces. When you have gotten your hand in on this netting work you'll be able to go right along. Let us emphasize, however, that speed is not the point—it is pleasure. Make your knots well, pull them up tightly. Your hands will get sore and you may want to tape up the places that take the brunt of the pulling.

IMPORTANT NOTE.   For the interest of those who would like to know how 39 inches was determined as correct for a 16-inch ring the following data is given as it may serve a useful purpose in figuring out variations in special nets that may be desired.

First determine the total length to be covered by hung netting. In the case of the landing net the diameter is used to get the circumference by multiplying 16 inches by 3.14 to get roughly an answer of 51 inches.

Actually a figure of 53 inches was arbitrarily used. Next determine how loosely you wish the net to hang. No looseness at all would mean that the net would be stretched tightly with no opening in the diamonds at all—obviously that would be ridiculous. But suppose that for every foot of hung netting you were to use 18 inches of stretched measure netting, obviously that would give a certain fullness to the hung net. The looser and fuller a net hangs the longer it wears and the less likelihood of disaster if a single strand breaks. For the basis of 18 inches of stretched netting to provide 12 inches of hung netting the term "hung on 1/3 basis" is used. For netting hung more loosely, that is, 24 inches of stretched netting to make 12 inches of hung netting the term "hung on ½ basis" is used. For the landing net here the author chose the ½ basis. In other words the stretched measure was to be twice the distance to be covered by hung netting. So—if we want 53 inches of hung netting, we shall have to have 106 inches of stretched netting. Each stretched mesh measured 2¾ inches (this is always fixed by the size gauge stick used), therefore dividing 106 by 2¾ we get 39 inches as the number of meshes required. For further particulars about netting fullness, explanation of stretched measure, etc., see page 47.

The Frame For Your Net

Shown on the top of the next page are three popular frames for boat landing nets. All are available at Netcraft. Style A is the type used on the broom stick handle of the net shown on page 16. This makes a good sturdy job and you'll like the way it handles in use. The lugs and ends are held in place by whipping over with twine,—see page 46, or by a metal sleeve, if you can find the right size.

If space is a big factor you'll enjoy a collapsible frame—Style B on next page which can now be had without the netting for attaching your own hand-made net bag. And another popular old time is Style C with the two-piece take-down handle. Its mouth opening is 15 inches but a 16-inch net will work on it.

If you want to add a fancy touch, put several inches of twine whipping at two convenient places where the hands naturally come on the handle. It insures a good safe grip. Shellac or varnish the whipping and it will stay on for keeps. Sheet cork, too, makes a fine grip—see Netcraft Cork Kit for details on spiral winding cork grips.

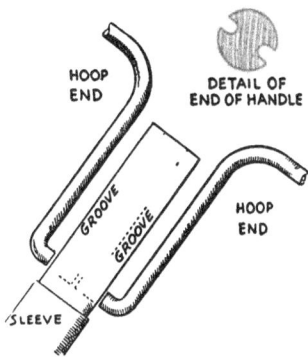

(A) LANDING NET RING

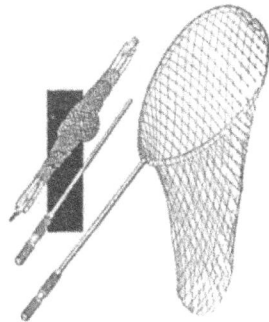

(B) COLLAPSIBLE FRAME

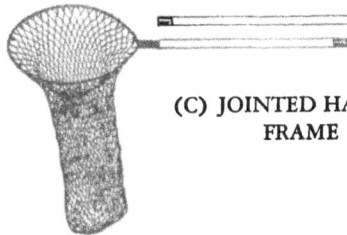

(C) JOINTED HANDLE FRAME

How To Make a Double Selvedge Edge

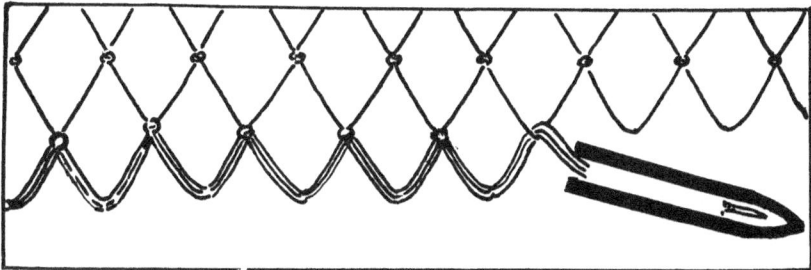

On landing nets, live bags, etc., it is often desirable to have the top edge stronger so as to take the wear. To do this make a row of meshes with a doubled twine. Simply load the shuttle with a length of twine doubled in two and do a row of knots in the usual manner, treating the doubled twine as though it were single. This can be done after the net is made and is ready to attach to the frame.

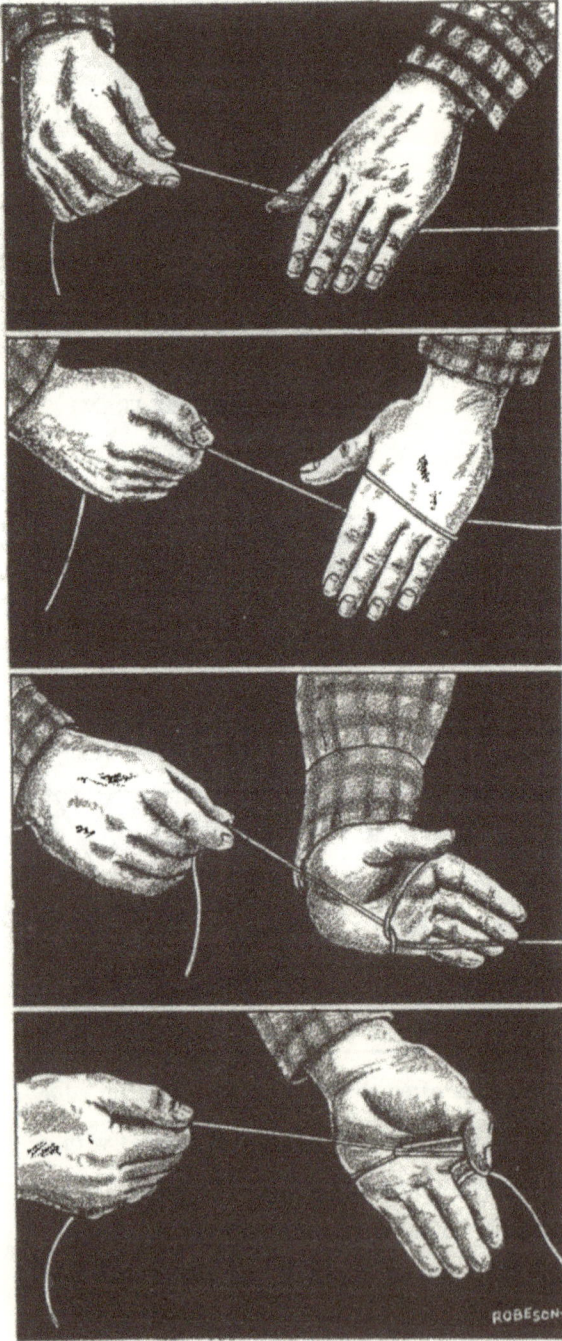

How To Break Twine

Learn This Valuable Little Trick

HOLD the free end in right hand and lay the left hand over the twine with palm down as shown in the top picture.

Next, make one wrap around left hand, as shown in the second picture.

Now turn the left hand fingers inside, toward stomach, and under by means of a simple circular motion of the wrist which now leaves the twine as shown in Fig. 3.

Turn the index finger of the left hand a couple of times around the stationary part of the twine which will thus lock that end and keep it from slipping. Now you simply draw up all the slack in the twine so that the whole thing appears as in the last picture, then with a quick hard jerk of the right hand the twine will readily break. A little practice and you have a most valuable trick—perhaps a bit lengthy to explain but in practice it takes only a second to do it.

OVERHAND WEAVING

For Working From
Right To Left

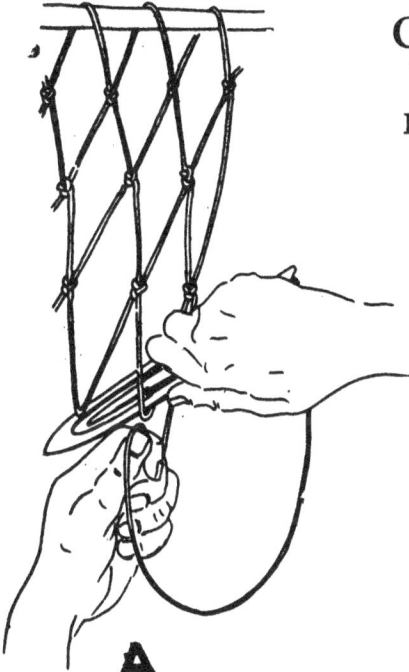

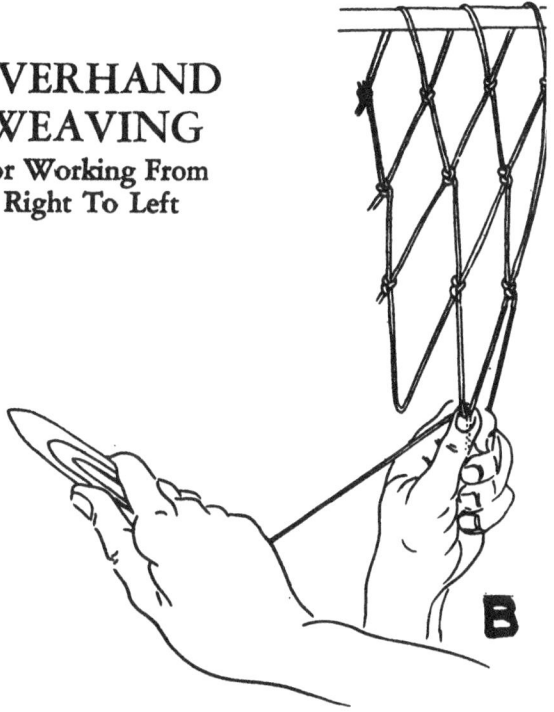

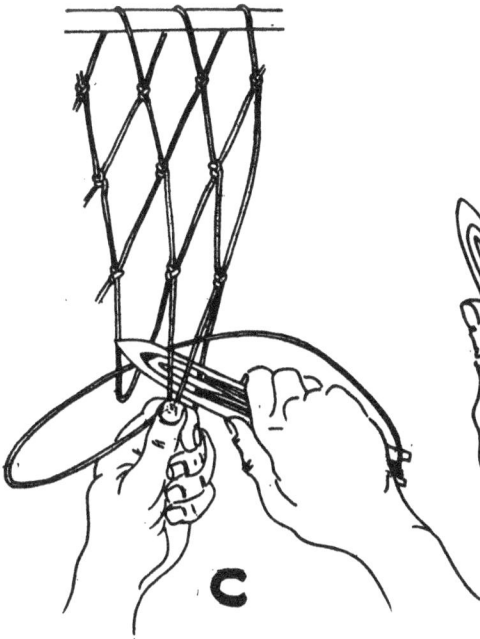

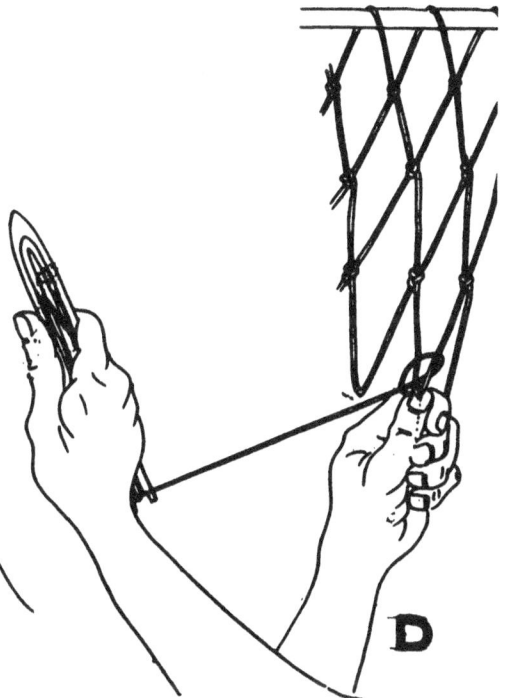

A

B

C

D

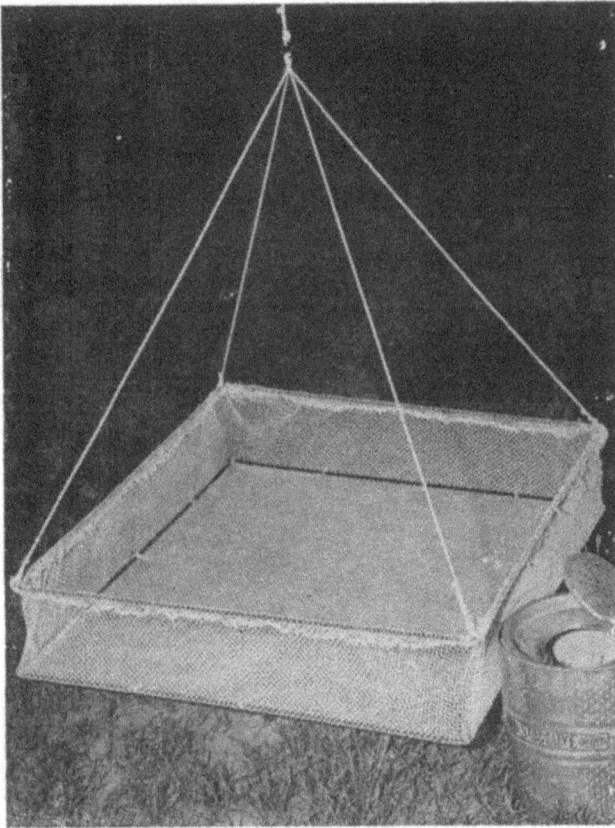

HOW TO MAKE A BASKET TYPE MINNOW NET

•

A One Evening
Project

•

F OR CATCHING minnows on inland lakes here is a net that has the author's heartiest recommendations. It works like a charm and what's more it is a one man affair. First let's see how it works.

You simply make up a dough by mixing oatmeal, flour and water. Butter two or three big chunks of this on the bottom meshes, leaving a ball of dough in the center. Locate likely minnow spots. They are mostly in the weeds near drop-off ledges. Patience and hard work in trying one spot after the other will be well repaid for once the bed is located you can usually take minnows there for the rest of the season, often for several seasons. This net is worked in water from 14 feet to 16 feet in depth—deep enough so minnows can't see the boat.

Let the baited net straight down over the side. It will completely collapse when on the bottom. Now let a handful of dry oatmeal filter down from the top—it will attract minnows from quite a distance. After a couple of minutes pull the net up hand over hand with a fairly fast, even lift.

The author has many times gotten a bucket full of minnows in one or two lifts. This is such a "honey" of a net that we urge every lake fisherman to make one—it will be one of your most treasured pieces of equipment. When minnows were not to be had at any price, we've taken them right out of the middle of the lake, on our selected spots, of course.

Surprising as it may seem, the net can be used right off the end of your dock. Most lakes have an abundance of shore minnows. These can be readily attracted to your dock by throwing out bread, oatmeal or food of some kind. You may never have seen a minnow around your dock but just get out some food, go away for an hour or so and most generally you'll find them there upon returning. Now you simply toss your net out flat (no bait in it yet),—the minnows, of course, will scatter. Then you throw oatmeal so that it will settle right over the net. When you have a nice bunch of minnows over the net, pull up quickly. What a thrilling sight—hundreds of flipping, jumping, wriggling minnows and right off your dock.

Note: The net in the picture was made merely by basting the netting over the frame. The following method is much better and more easily managed.

One piece of netting makes the entire basket and sides. It is ¼" knotted minnow netting that hangs four feet deep and when gathered rope like and stretched with about a two-pound pull, the piece is cut to a length of 53 inches.

Tie one end of a 12-foot length of No. 21 twine to the 15th mesh in from one corner, counting on the diagonal from the corner toward the opposite corner. Now with the other end of this cord threaded on a large needle, baste this cord in and out through each successive mesh toward the edge, making the needle some out about 14 inches from the nearest corner. Now continue basting, following along one side, until you come to a point 14 inches away (stretched measure) from the next corner. At this point you start rounding the corner instead of going around a square corner. Make the needle pass through the 15th mesh in from that corner and at this point pull the basting cord tight (not the netting,—just the basting cord) and tie it to the 15th mesh so that the basting cord is exactly 30 inches long from the starting knot.

Continue to the next corner the same way, round the corner 14 inches from the corner and tie again to the 15th mesh as before, again making the basting cord 30 inches from the last knot. Continue this way until you have completely basted the netting with the strong cord and the starting and finishing ends are tied together. Now trim off the excess netting where you have rounded the corners.

Take two 80" lengths of No. 84 seine twine and thread on a 1" iron ring, then tie the four ends to the four corners of a frame—30" square made of 3/16 steel, butt welded and enameled.   (Continued on Page 40.)

HOW TO MAKE
A CAMPING HAMMOCK

H ERE IS a hammock designed for the sportsman—plenty big, plenty strong and easy to roll up and carry anywhere. You can make the entire hammock, including the fancy attachment to the rings and the braided sides.

Materials needed are: 2 lbs. of No. 60 soft twine, 2 iron hammock rings, 2 spreader sticks 1"x2"x31"long. Note: The entire job can be made of No. 60 soft but if you have some No. 72 twine we suggest using that for the end cords that attach to the iron rings. Use a Jumbo shuttle and a gauge that makes a four-inch stretched measure mesh.

Using the method described on Page 12 for doing netting in the flat, make 20 starting loops which is done by doing 40 knots on the starting chain. Transfer these loops to a stiff rod supported across two nails. You now have the first TWO rows done as shown on the chart. The third row is Regular, that is, it is done exactly as shown in pictures 10 and 11 on Page 12.

Now the fourth row is Double. This is done by passing the shuttle around the gauge stick TWICE instead of once.

The fifth row is single gage with an extra mesh inserted between the 6th and 7th loops and the 14th and 15th. This increasing stunt is illustrated on Page 15, Figure 12.

Now simply follow the chart showing how each row is to be made. Next you'll need two braided side ropes. Please refer to Page 28 showing how this braiding is done using four cords. The complete braided cord when stretched tight from end loop to end loop should be 5½ inches shorter than the stretched length of the body of the hammock measured between two ends about four loops in from the side edge. By having the braided lines shorter it gives support to the sides and lets the middle stretch out.

Drill 20 evenly spaced 3/16" holes on the 2" face of the spreader stick. Tie the outside rigging lines from braided ropes to the rings (each of these lines is double), then tie each rigging line to its respective loop of the hammock. The sides are attached to the braiding by "sewing" with No. 60 soft twine and attaching each side loop at two points on the braided line. Use a nail to open up the braiding and use your fingers to push the line through. Where your "sewing" line goes through a side loop do not tie a knot but just let it slide free.

After you have taken some of the stretch out of the hammock you'll need some of the rigging lines.

In the illustration at the right you'll notice that a reference line leads from the cut to the type.

Row	Gage	Instructions
1	Single	The first two rows are
2	Single	made by the starting chain
3	Single	Regular
4	Double	Go twice around gage
5	Single	Increase between 6 & 7; 14 & 15
6	Single	Regular
7	Double	Go twice around gage
8	Double	Go twice around gage
9	Single	Increase between 3 & 4; 20 & 21
10	Single	Regular
11	Double	Go twice around gage
12	Single	Increase between 5 & 6; 19 & 20
13	Single	Reuglar
14	Double	Go twice around gage
15	Single	Regular
16	Single	Regular
17	Double	Go twice around gage
18	Single	Regular
19	Single	Knit 5 & 6 together; also 19 & 20
20	Double	Go twice around gage
21	Single	Regular
22	Single	Knit 3 & 4 together; also 20 & 21
23	Double	Go twice around gage
24	Double	Go twice around gage
25	Single	Regular
26	Single	Knit 6 & 7 together; also 14 & 15
27	Double	Go twice around gage
28	Single	Regular
29	Single	Regular
30	Single	No knots, loops are hanging there

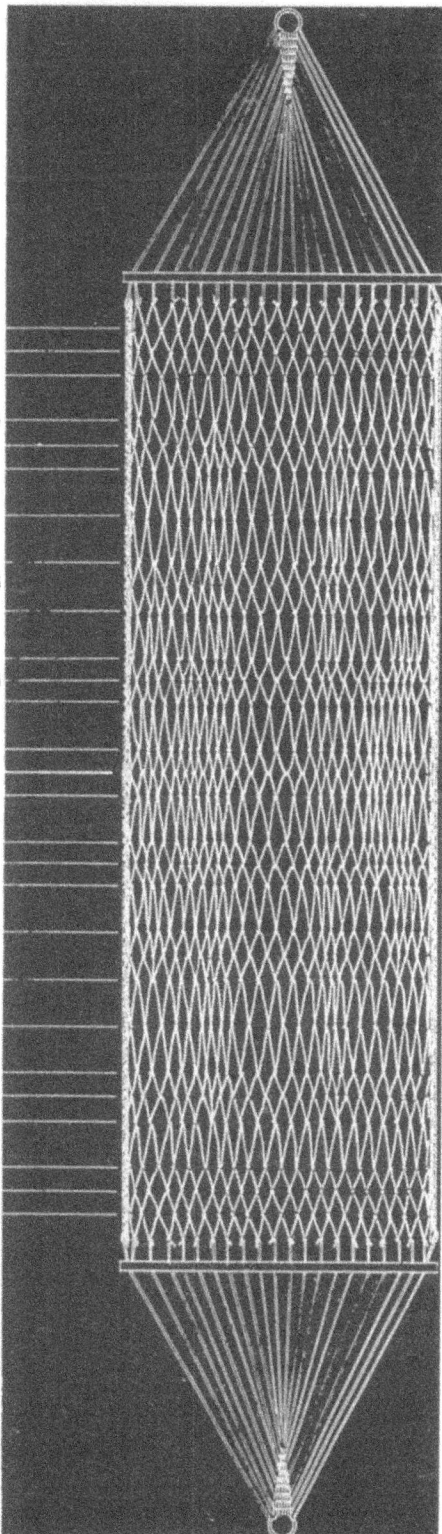

HOW TO DO FOUR-CORD BRAIDING

In braiding, whatever length you want finished cord to be add ¼ more which is taken up in the braiding. For the hammock, the four cords should be 100 inches long,— two loops 200 inches long. Tie a loop as shown above and hang it on a nail. The braiding is done by passing the right cord over ONE cord and hold in position by pinching.
Then pass the left cord over TWO cords and pinch. Then back to the outermost cord on the right passing it over ONE cord as before, then the left over TWO. Continue that way—Right over One, Left over TWO, and you have the beautiful braiding as shown. At the end, tie two pairs into knots to keep from slipping, then tie a loop to make the bottom the same as the top. The dotted lines of the right hand view merely shows where the right hand cord will be after passing over one cord.

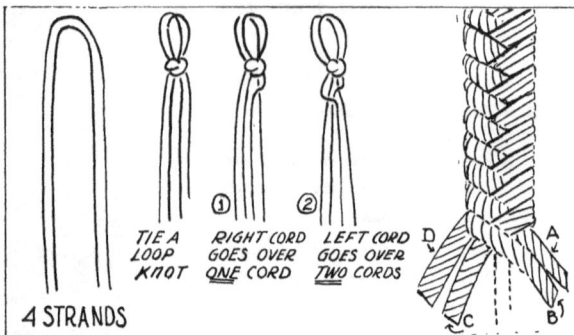

How To Make a Fancy Hammock Attachment To Ring

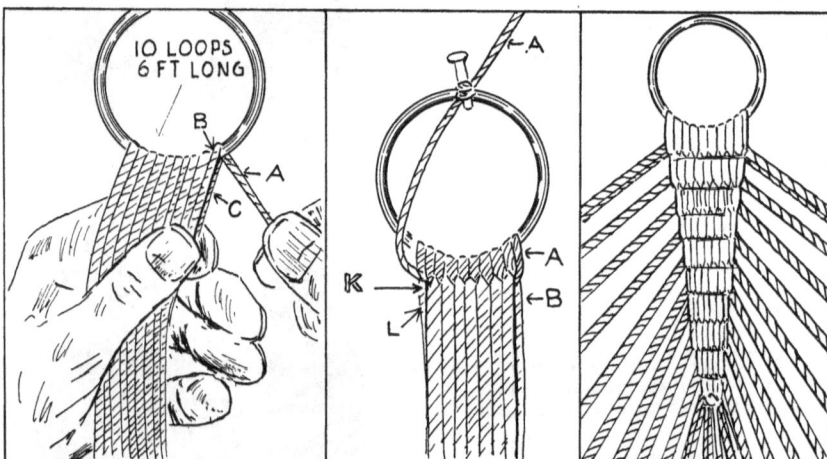

Start with 10 loops of cord (60 soft is O. K., but use 72 if you have it) and pass these loops over your ring as shown. Flatten into orderly position as shown, holding the cords with left hand. It is a simple weaving trick. Take the REAR right cord,—this will be the "threading" cord. Pass it OVER its front cord, marked "B," then BEHIND the next appearing back cord, marked "C," then OVER the front cord, behind a back cord, and so on. Continue weaving the "threading" cord "A" that way until it comes out at "K" from whence it is to be tied to a nail. Then put your left finger clear through at "K" and pull the leftmost cord marked "L" all the way through to the right and tie at the nail the same as cord "A." At this point insert one extra six foot cord right through that same passage way

(Continued On Page 49)

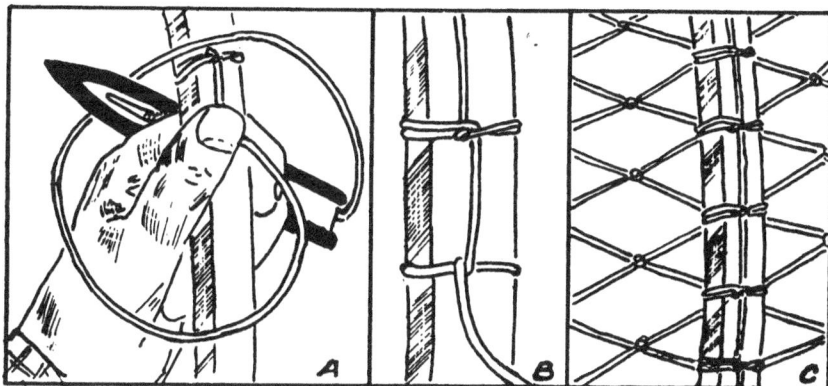

HOW TO ATTACH NETS TO HOOPS

THESE instructions are sketched, above, for wooden hoops but the method is the same for wire hoops and also it applies to landing nets, turtle traps, in fact, any netting fastened tightly to a hoop. In turtle traps and fish traps it is essential to tie the netting to hoops. In small horizontally held netting like on clamp-on bags, etc., you can simply slip the netting on the hoop from an open end, if you wish.

The knot used is two half hitches, tied one over the other. In large mesh work you can tie every second or third mesh, merely letting the shuttle pass through each mesh of the ones not to be securely tied.

The position in which you work is important. Sit down. Hold the hoop between the knees and work TOWARD you. The whole trick in fastening nets to hoops is in SPACING the meshes. A practical way is to tie any mesh to the hoop, then count half way around your meshes and tie again at the opposite side of the hoop. Then, take each half, if you wish, and tie at the quarter marks using ordinary square knots and pieces of string to temporarily hold the netting. This will give you somewhat of an idea how far apart the ties will come. Another way to get the distance between ties is to divide the circumference (circumference is 3.14 times the diameter) by your total number of meshes to be hung. Mark this distance on your shuttle edge by using black marks on a piece of white tape. With a practical "eye" you can later judge the distance between meshes.

Start by tying your loaded shuttle string tightly to hoop. The knot you can see by the pictures. The netting is allowed to hang on the under side of the hoop. The thumb and first finger of the left hand hold the tie string AND THE MESH TO BE TIED, in place, then two half hitches does the trick to hold the mesh secure. The meshes can be straightened out in neat diamond pattern after the job is through. When you get within three or four meshes of one of your quarter or half-way marks check with your eye to see if you are coming out even. If you are going to be "long" then shorten each spacing a little. If too much off it is best to go back and do it over.

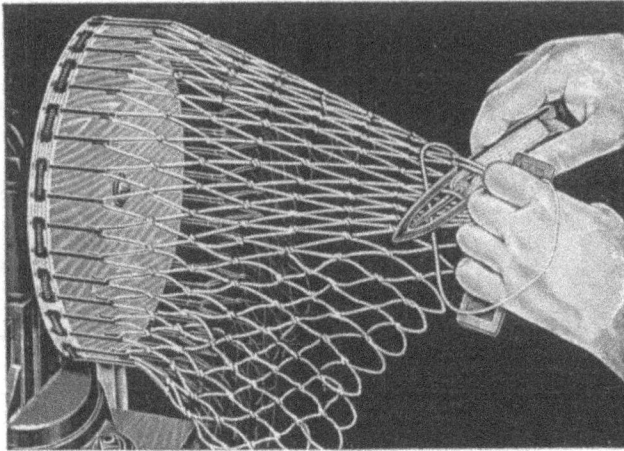

HOW TO USE THE NETCRAFT WHEEL

Enjoy This New, Fascinating Way of Making Nets Without Seams

The Netcraft Wheel is a special device that enables you to do continuous tubular netting work without seams. While the wheel is only 10 inches in diameter it will handle any size mesh, thus making possible a tube or web of netting. Obviously such a shape is ideal for speedily making such things as landing nets, live bags, turtle traps, hoop nets, in fact, any net of tubular or bag shape. There are 40 hooks on the wheel making possible 40 starting meshes and as the meshes may be large ones the circumference that the finished net will cover may be 30 inches or more. Also, the number of meshes may be increased, after making the first two rows, so that there is a wide range of size.

To use the wheel you should first know how to make the netting knot as described on Page 12. Practice this knot several times before starting work on the wheel. To begin, the wheel must first be solidly mounted to withstand quite a hard pulling strain. The mounting may be done in one of several ways: (1) clamp the handle in a solidly mounted wood or machine vise, (2) screw handle to wall, (3) strap handle with web straps to edge of door or any heavy piece of furniture, bed post, or upright. Sketch A shows web strap pulled up tightly around door knobs to hold wheel to edge of door, the door being held rigid by wedging in a rubber door holder, one on each side.

ATTACHING STARTING LOOPS

Select the size mesh you want to make and have handy the mesh gage. Load your shuttle with twine but leave about three feet hanging loose at the end which will not be wound on the shuttle. This is called "the loose end." Now hook your twine on to any one of the protruding wheel hooks, allowing the three foot loose end to dangle free at the left. See Sketch B. Pass the twine over the gage and hook on to each successive hook as shown. Remove the gage after each two or three loops so as to easily work from loop to loop. The spring tension of each hook should keep each loop from slipping. After the second row around the wheel you'll need to give no further thought to the twine slipping on the hooks.

TIE LOOSE END AT TERMINATION OF EACH ROW. This is important:—When you have cast on all the loops, tie the ends together as shown in Sketch C. Thus you now have all the starting loops alike and a long "loose end" still remaining. It is important to retain this loose end for each time you go around the wheel and get back to your starting point you will tie on to the loose end to complete each individual circle or "collar" of meshes.

See Sketch D—Now you're on your way with the second row by holding your gage in the left hand and making the regular netting meshes with which you are already familiar—as shown in Figures 3, 4, and 5 of Page 12. Always work from left to right and after a few meshes slip the gage out and continue on. When you have a few rows on the wheel the work becomes easier and more meshes may be left on the gage before removing it.

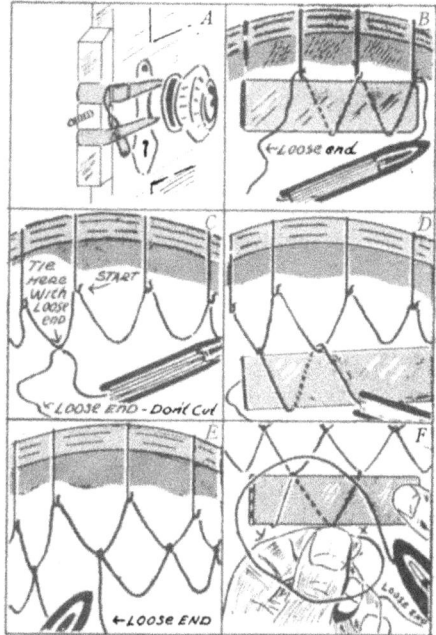

Now we'll say you've gone around the second time and you are about to bring the shuttle end together with the loose end as in Sketch E. Here is how that tie is made. Let go your shuttle, and holding the gage in the RIGHT hand, pinch the two cords together with thumb and forefinger of left hand as in Figure F to make a uniform mesh. While still pinching, remove the gage and make a netting knot by passing shuttle behind point "X" and come up through at "Y." Then REPEAT this knot again to make it well secured. Now proceed on to the next row, still leaving that loose end to close the next row of meshes.

REDUCING AND ENLARGING

To reduce or taper a web, as in making a landing net, simply gather two meshes at a time as shown in Figure

13, Page 15 in the section on general netting instructions. To enlarge or add meshes to a row you will also find this work shown on Page 15.

TO MAKE A DOUBLE EDGE. This is not difficult and is often done to give greater strength at point of most wear. You simply thread your shuttle with two threads instead of one and after a net is all done, for example a landing net, hang it up by the tail on a nail, and work in one more circle of knots using the double thread exactly as though it were single.

PROJECT DETAILS

LANDING NET. Materials: No. 12 Medium Twine or No. 16 Soft Twine (easier on hands and ties secure knots), Medium Shuttle, Medium Gage, Landing Net Frame, ¾" Bone Ring. Make 16 rows, each row being full 40 inches around. Each row thereafter, make a Reduction (gather two in one) at two different places in each row. Thus in each row you will lose two meshes. Stagger these Reductions so they do not all come directly beneath each other. Continue making these Reductions until you have only 20 loops showing on the web. Make one more row without any reduction, then close these 20 loops on a bone ring, as described on Page 18.

Note: You can easily design your landing net to suit your needs. To make it longer — simply add more rows. You'll observe, too, that the more rows you make before Reducing, the fuller the net will hang — a quality seldom found in nets you buy at the stores.

LIVE NET DETAIL. Material: No. 9 or No. 12 Medium Twine, No. 2 Gage, Sardine Shuttle, a 10-inch Clamp-On Frame for attaching to boat. Make 38 starting loops by omitting two hooks when casting on the starting row. Continue the web until the desired depth is secured. Do not taper this type of net until near the bottom, then lose four meshes per row until there are but 16 or 18 meshes left. Make one last row without any reductions, then attach the last loops to a ¾" bone ring by the method previously described.

FISH TRAPS. Since the "sock" or web part can be made any size on the Netcraft Wheel and any length is had by continuing the mesh work to desired size, you can see that it is possible to make about any kind of hoop net you may fancy. Here are a few hints: (1) Decide on your stretched mesh size and the size of the hoop. (2) Get the number of starting meshes by dividing the stretched mesh size into twice the circumference. Example: A 3½ inch stretched mesh on a 21-inch ring (66 inches around) would require 38 starting meshes. If the number of starting meshes needed is more than the number of hooks, then cast on the 40 starting loops and do the increasing stunt as in Figure 12, until you have the required number of loops.

A funnel may be made at any point on the web, after the web is completed. The trick is to tie on at the desired point where the funnel is to go and weave a row of meshes right on to the main web. Continue going around and around weaving what will eventually be a collar on the outside of the main web. Now when the whole affair is turned INSIDE OUT you'll have your funnel. To make the funnel tapered, reduce the number of meshes. Finally, finish the funnel into a solid ring as shown for the turtle traps but tie it open at four points instead of two, thus it is not necessary to have any rings for the small end of the funnels.

Clyde Weirick, Veteran Trapper, With Two Fine Snappers

TURTLE TRAP MADE ON THE NETCRAFT WHEEL. In this method of making turtle traps, the entire web including the entrance funnel and tail part are all made in one piece. It comes out beautifully — no seams and after some experience you'll be able to make good time in completing a trap. Of course the more traps you set at a time the better your chances for a big take of turtles. Material: No. 21 Medium or No. 20 Soft Twine. (Soft twine has same strength as medium but is easier on hands and knots jam up easily.) A Mesh Gage to make 5-inch Stretched Measure, and a Mesh Gage to make 4-inch Stretched Measure, a Super Long Shuttle, Medium Shuttle and three 27-inch diameter rings.

Using the No. 5 gage, cast on 38 starting loops by omitting two hooks on the wheel. Now continue with the same gage and make 20 rows of knots, that means—go around the wheel 20 times. This will give you a hoop or web 10 meshes deep by 38 meshes around. This makes the barrel part that covers the three equally spaced hoops.

Next comes the tail part. After making the 20 rows mentioned above continue right on but change to a No. 4 Mesh Gage and tie on to only every other mesh. See Sketch G. In other words, go from X to Y, skipping the mesh in between. Another thing, instead of going once around this gage as you were doing previously, you make TwO passes around the gage before

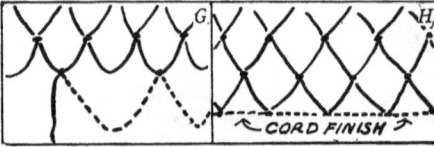

making each tie. This gives you an 8-inch stretched mesh for the end which allows fish to pass through the trap. Now when you start your second row of this large mesh work, do not skip any meshes but knot each mesh in succession. Go seven times around the wheel in this large mesh work, including the first row. This makes the end 3½ meshes deep.

Next, remove the net from wheel and rehook the tail end to the wheel, using only every other hook. The entrance funnel is to be 3½ meshes deep, of the same size mesh as the tail part. So you simply tie on to any one of the smaller starting loops and do large mesh work (twice around the 4-inch gage) until you have gone around the wheel seven times. Now you close the entrance into a ring by tying a single cord at points 1, 2, 3, 4, etc., as shown by the dotted line in Figure H. Use the regular netting knot for this operation.

The web is now all in one piece and to fasten it to the hoops follow directions given in this manual entitled—"Fastening Hoop Webs to Hoops." The tail piece is gathered together with one pucker string. The funnel or entrance is made by turning the front end inward and tie with two strings to the nearest hoop as pictures in this manual.

EXPLANATION OF PICTURES

The net at the lower right is exactly what you get if you follow instructions given here. The entire web, including funnel and tail part, is all in one piece. The hat shows where Mr. Turtle goes in and it also gives you an idea of relative size.

The upper picture is included memerly to give you a better idea how the funnel is rigged.

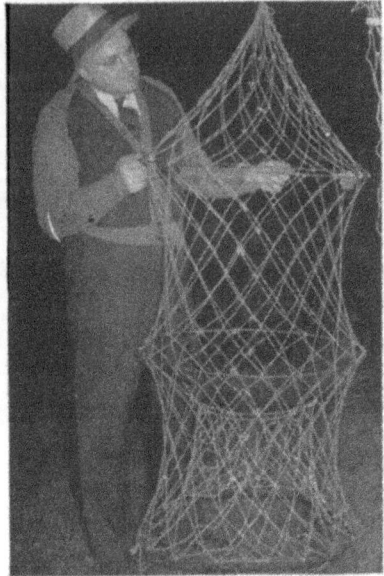

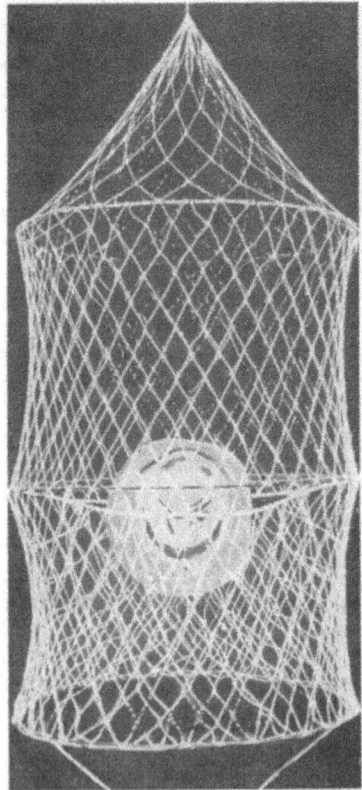

A WORD ABOUT TURTLE TRAPPING

TURTLE trapping is becoming increasingly popular. The beginners start out with a trap or two and the old-timers set a whole string of traps. The wroter accompanied Clyde Weirick on a trip in which over 300 pounds of turtles were caught in one night, using about 40 traps exactly like the one shown in the lower view of opposite page. One trap alone had four big snappers.

The trap is held horizontally by two stakes in shallow water so that a few inches of the trap sticks above water. The trap is baited with fish or chicken scraps tied in a loose mesh bag supported in the center of the trap by cords attached to the rings. The turtles scent the fish oil, so always face your trap down stream or away from shore so the turtle will be presented with the mouth of the trap as he approaches his "meal." Turtle trapping is usually done at night and it is best in warm weather. Take along gunny sacks to bring 'em back.

And Boy! Talk about your great eatin', you're sure in for a treat. You'll find the turtle is just as good eatin' as chicken,—no wild taste, no fishy taste. The meat is firm and of pleasing texture—looks appetizing too, the four leg joints being somewhat like chicken drum sticks. Rolled in flour and fried like chicken—take it from me, you really have something. Of course, turtle soup needs no special plug—a rare delicacy in fashionable restaurants, it'll make a hit with the family and friends.

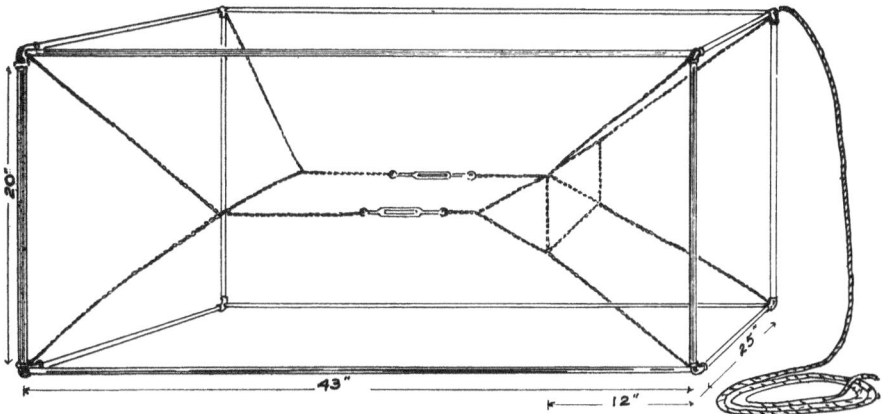

Pipe Frame For Turtle Trap or Live Box

My inventor friend, O. A. Friemoth, has a turtle trap made of 1/8″ galvanized pipe. He has caught plenty of turtles with it and if you are handy with pipe you can't go wrong with this design. It is too expensive for the fellow who wants a "string" of traps. The one big advantage, however, is that no stakes are required and you can use this trap without going in the water—simply throw it in—(notice that the tie rope is fastened to one corner).

The two end frames are tightened up solid but the four side pieces of pipe are removable so you have quick take-down and little space required. Tension between the ends is achieved by ordinary screen door turn-buckles rigged on to the pipes as shown with the type chain used in furnace controls. Fasten the chain to the corner "Ls" with pieces of wire. All this rigging is adjusted before going on the trip; on location you have only to get the four side pipes in place. These side pipes have no threads but rest between bolts ($\frac{1}{4}$"x1$\frac{1}{4}$" long) that have been screwed into the corner "Ls" by first drilling and then threading.

The work is best done on a Netcraft Wheel using the same method as described for the round turtle traps. The netting that stretches over the frame is 20 meshes around by 11$\frac{1}{2}$ meshes long. The mesh size is six-inch stretched measure, No. 24 twine. The funnel part is six meshes deep using a 3$\frac{1}{2}$" stretched measure gage tied as a continuous part of the main frame webbing by the method pictured in "G," top of page 34 and described in the instructions for making the round turtle trap. In knitting the funnel reduce one mesh each row so that the end is only 15 meshes around. Do the cord finish stunt (See Figure H, Page 34) but use chain instead of cord and half hitch the chain to the netting with seine twine at each point of contact.

The back end of the trap may be woven on the wheel, also as a continuous piece of the main body, done on a wheel. Simply reduce the mesh size to 3$\frac{1}{2}$" stretched measure, catch every other mesh as shown in "G," Page 34, and knit 3$\frac{1}{2}$ meshes deep, reducing three meshes in each row. A single pucker string passed through all the end loops pulls the end of the net closed like a drum head and makes for easy opening to get turtles out.

MAKE A GENUINE SOUTH SEAS CAST NET

O F ALL THE advanced net making projects this is about the most interesting,—a real South Seas Cast Net. While it looks tough it really isn't,—just takes time, and that's good for there's hours and hours of real pleasure making this affair (over 20,000 knots). This is the net you've read about, or possibly have seen first hand, used by the native islanders all over the world and occasionally seen along our own shores— especially the Gulf Coast and Florida. (Continued On Page 38)

two rows are made with your shuttle threaded double, that is, wound two threads on shuttle together but used as a single thread. The last row should also be of doubled thread. Starting with the third row you do the widening trick,—see Figure 12, Page 12. These wideners, called Risers, are put at 11 evenly spaced places around the row. Make the first Riser come two knots to the right of the "loose end" or tie string.

After you have made this row having 11 wideners then make two regular rows without wideners. And now here is an important detail—EVERY THIRD ROW GETS 11 WIDENERS OR RISERS AND THEY SHOULD ALL COME EXACTLY UNDER THE PREVIOUS 11 RISERS. To make this possible and to keep the tie string closing of each row from crossing the line of Risers, it is necessary to knit EVERY OTHER ROW on the INSIDE of the netting instead of the outside. The picture in this book of the Netcraft Wheel shows the hand knitting on the outside—now to knit on the inside, just drop the hand down to the BOTTOM of the wheel and knit from left to right as usual.

The lead line should be about 3/16" cotton—this is a No. 84 seine twine or No. 96 twine. The leads are attached, as shown, using No. 16 soft twine. It will help to have one end of the lead line tied to a hook or something while attaching the leads. (Continued On Page 40)

The principle of the cast net is simply this: The weights around the outside quickly sink the 17-foot diameter net over the fish and the 22 brail lines attached to a 30-foot hand line, made of sash cord, cause the net to pouch or bag around the trapped fish. One end of the hand line is tied to the wrist to leave both hands free to 'trow the net. The net is used both to catch bait fish and edible fish.

You probably won't find a cast net maker within ten counties but rest assured there are brother net makers and Boy! what enthusiastic "nuts" they are in this rare hobby. There is nothing else like it—but don't expect to make 15 pounds of net and leads pancake out flat for you the first time. It'll take practice.

The drawings contain essential details. You'll need two ¾-pound spools of No. 20/9 Sea Island Cotton twine. Nothing else will really do the job as well. It is soft and silky, ties easily and it's very long fibers give it real strength to stand dragging over rocks and ledges. A Netcraft Wheel is essential for it now relieves the difficulty of seams and enables an amateur to get started with least trouble. By the way, don't make the cast net as your first project, do something else first—get acquainted with "enlarging" and tying the netting knot with some speed.

There are altogether 102 rows of knots. The first

REQUIRED —

SEA ISLAND COTTON NO 20/9
13 LBS OF 1 OZ LEADS
METAL THIMBLE
NO 1 SWIVEL
3/16" LEAD LINE
1 LB NO 16 SOFT TWINE
SARDINE SHUTTLE
GAGE - 2" MESH (stretched)
NETCRAFT WHEEL

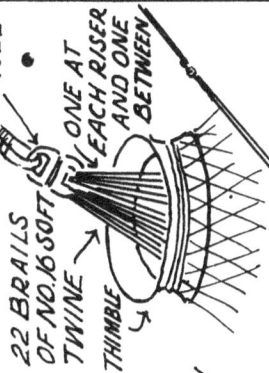

SWIVEL

22 BRAILS
OF NO.16 SOFT
TWINE

ONE AT
EACH RISER
AND ONE
BETWEEN

THIMBLE

33 STARTING MESHES
WHEEL HOOKS

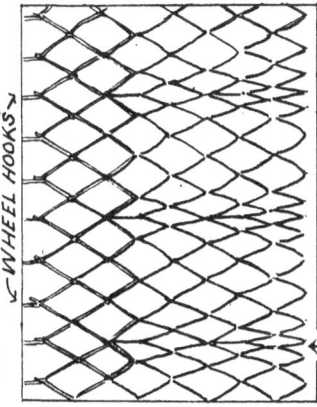

STARTING WITH THE THIRD
ROW, AT 11 PLACES AROUND
THE NET INSERT "RISERS" OR
INCREASES. NOTICE HOW THE
RISERS COME DIRECTLY BELOW
EACH OTHER WITH TWO ROWS
BETWEEN MADE PLAIN WITHOUT
ANY RISERS, THUS THE NET
GETS 11 MESHES BIGGER EVERY
THIRD TIME AROUND UNTIL THE
LAST ROW HAS A TOTAL
OF 396 MESHES

FISH ARE TRAPPED HERE
WHEN NET IS THROWN
FLAT LIKE
THIS
AND RETRIEVED

DIA. 17 FT.

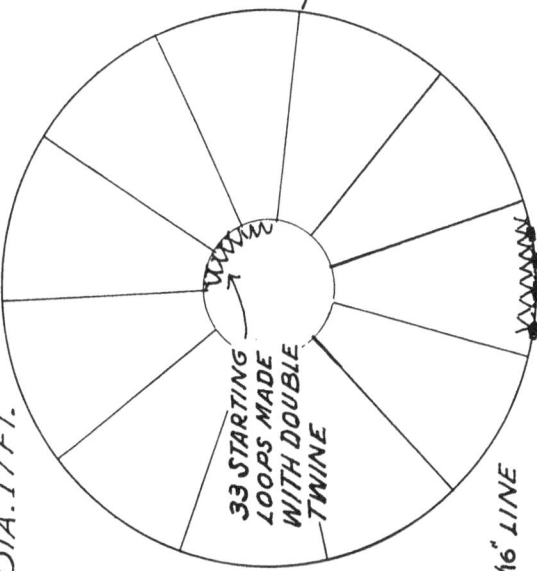

33 STARTING
LOOPS MADE
WITH DOUBLE
TWINE

3/16" LINE

1 OZ LEADS ATTACHED
AS SHOWN BELOW

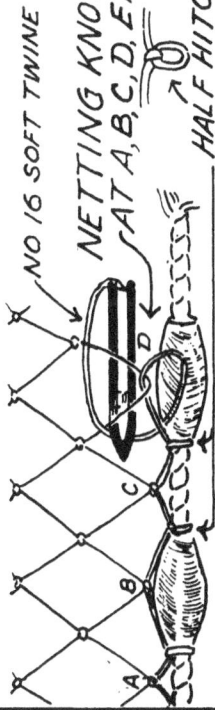

NO 16 SOFT TWINE

NETTING KNOTS
AT A, B, C, D, ETC.

HALF HITCHES

A   B   C   D

Make a Genuine South Seas Cast Net
(Continued From Page 38)

Next, attach the starting loops to the outside of the special thimble, as shown, using No. 16 soft twine—whip over securely. Now attach the 28 brails, or "pucker" lines,—one for each line of Risers and one between. Attach them on the under side so they permit the net to flatten out. The brails are atached to a swivel which permits the net to turn when cast.

Do not be disturbed over any slight variation in your net. The diameter of 17 feet will vary according to the material used and the way the knots are pulled up. The value of your net will increase with use. Such nets are not for sale and are all strictly hand made. Their very rarity and unique, primitive method of catching fish add greatly to their interest and fun both in making and using. Go to it, and please send us a snap shot.

How To Make a Basket Type Minnow Net
(Continued From Page 25)

Slide the ring until it is centered and hang the whole affair on a nail overhead.

Now tie four 10" pieces of No. 60 soft twine to the same four corners of the same frame and use these four tie strings to now tie the four corners of your basted netting to the four corners of the top frame. If you have measured carefully the basting cord 30" long will lay alongside each side of the frame without any slack.

Next drop the other square frame in place to form the bottom but do not tie in place as yet. Exert same pressure on the bottom frame to create a uniform side wall. (It helps in exerting even tension on this bottom frame to let a two-pound weight of some kind hang by four cords to the center of each side of the bottom frame.)

The entire top edge of the netting and basting cord is now to be lashed to the top frame. For this purpose use No. 16 soft twine and a large needle. Tie securely at one corner, then every two inches tie a half hitch and at every third tying point make two half hitches, one over the other. Thus you go all around the top securing the net to the frame with one continuous cord.

The bottom frame is tied in place with little tie strings, four on each side, or a total of 16 tie strings. If your state laws do not permit use of net with a side wall, simply untie the bottom frame and leave it out.

Your net is now complete except for a little whipping a few inches below the iron ring to keep it from slipping. Also you'll need about 20 feet of 1/4" rope for lowering and hauling in the net. For safety, tie a float on end of rope in case net should drop overboard unattended.

NETTING MESH SIZE—How To Measure

FROM the picture at the left you will notice that the size of a mesh may be given either as the length of one of the "square" legs, or it may be given in terms of the length from one knot to an opposite knot,—when the mesh is stretched out tight. Of course when it is stretched out tight there will be no opening showing in the "diamond" and so naturally the stretched measure is simply twice the square measure. In speaking of a mesh size as being for example two inches, it is therefore plain that one must know whether you mean stretched or square measure. The method of making the double selvage illustrated here is shown in detail on page 27.

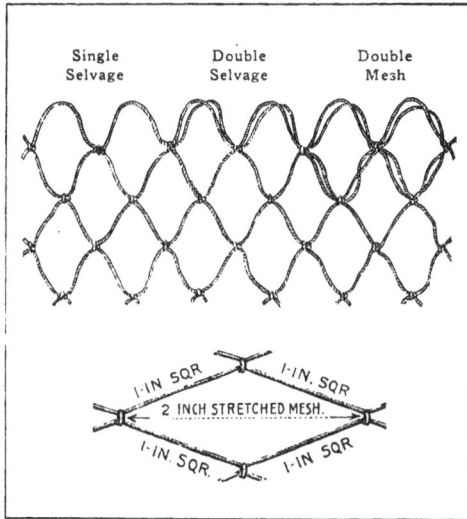

How To Obtain Fullness in Hanging Nets

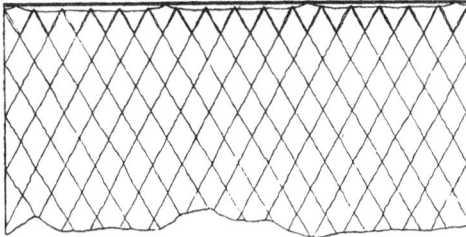

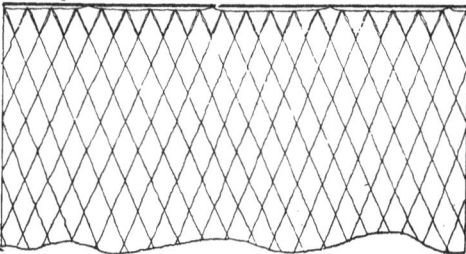

The fullness of a net when attached to its support is determined by how closely bunched or how spread out the meshes are when attached. The middle picture of this page shows a net hung on ½ basis which means that for every 12 inches of hung netting there was 24 inches of stretched measure netting used. The bottom picture shows a net hung on 1/3 basis which means that for each 12 inches of hung netting there are 18 inches of stretched netting used. On the following page is a table of various fullnesses in use.

One quarter ....(1/4) basis is 16 inches to the foot.
One-third ....(1/3) basis is 18 inches to the foot.
Two-fifths ....(2/5) basis is 20 inches to the foot.
Three-sevenths ....(3/7) basis is 21 inches to the foot.
One-half ....(1/2) basis is 24 inches to the foot.
Five-ninths ....(5/9) basis is 27 inches to the foot.
Three-fifths ....(3/5) basis is 30 inches to the foot.

HOW SEINE TWINE SIZE MAY BE DETERMINED.   It is important to every net maker to be able to examine a piece of seine twine and determine what size it is. Perhaps you might wish to copy a certain net after examining it and naturally the first consideration is—what size twine?

All seine twine is a twist of three main cables. Each cable has a certain number of threads in it, therefore to get the total thread count you simply multiply the thread count of a single cable by three. For example, you examine a piece of twine and separate one of the three main cables and by reverse twisting this single cable you plainly count four separate threads, then the total count is 12 and you call this 12-thread or simply No. 12 seine twine.

Twines are twisted loosely, more firmly, or quite tight. The loosely twisted twine is called "Soft Laid," the more firmly twisted is called "Medium Laid" or simply "Medium," and the tightly twisted is called "Hard Laid." The twine most commonly used is Medium Laid.

Seine twine is best used from a skein rather than a ball. Most commercial fishermen prefer the skeins as the twine lays straighter without as many kinks as ball twine. Skeins should be kept stretched between two spikes as soon as unpacked.

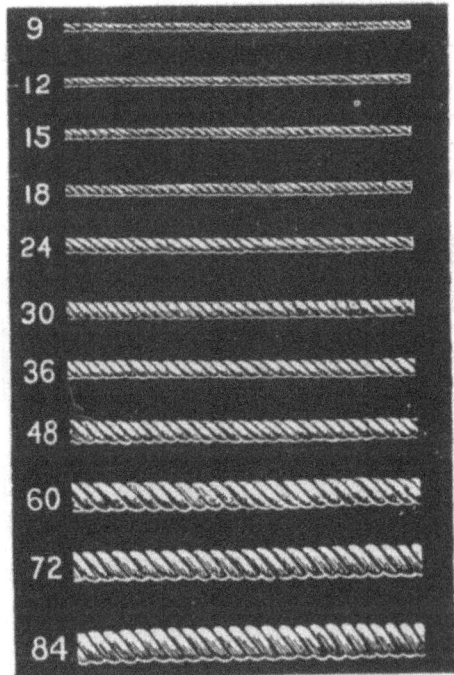

IMPORTANT INFORMATION
Regarding the Making of Minnow Netting and Small Mesh Work

THE SMALLEST mesh that it is practical to make using Netcraft shuttles is 1½" stretched measure. This size calls for a Sardine shuttle and 1½" gage. You can make ¼" (square measure) work but it is not practical because the work is extremely slow and tedious. For those who, nevertheless, wish to try it, AND WHO HAVE FIRST LEARNED TO DO LARGE MESH WORK WITH GOOD SPEED, here are a few tips: First you'll need a special gage about as thin as a thin dime and about ¼" wide. Make this out of cigar box wood and sandpaper it smooth. Follow the same procedure in making a starting chain and all other operations as explained on page 12. Instead of a rod to hold the starting chain of meshes use a steel crotchet needle or eight-inch mattress needle. Instead of a shuttle, simply use a heavy darning needle and let about three or four feet of twine threaded on the needle be pulled through each time you tie a knot. It is tedious work but it can be done. Use No. 20/6 Sea Island Cotton or No. 20/9 Sea Island Cotton. Regular seine twine is far too heavy for these tiny knots. In tying the knot you won't be able to stick your index finger alongside the "V" as in larger work so you simply let the flat of your thumb hold the "V" and as the knot is tightened let the thumb "roll" the knot into place so that it won't tighten below the "V" as cautioned about on Page 12, Figure 7.

———•———

HOW TO MAKE A PULLMAN TYPE CLOTHES HAMMOCK

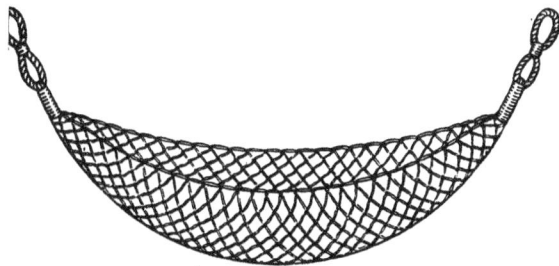

HERE IS a handy hammock like the ones used in Pullman berths. Every sportsman can use one—works fine in a tent, boat, car or trailer to hold clothes or miscellaneous objects. Makes a fine toy hammock too for a youngster.

Use either No. 9 or No. 12 Netcraft Seine Twine. The mesh size is 2" stretched. Start with five meshes (11 knots on the starting chain) and thread these onto a holding stick just as described for making a landing net. Somewhere in EACH of the first 15 rows add an extra mesh. At the end of the fifteenth row the net will be 20 meshes wide at the center. Somewhere in each of the next 15 rows decrease by one knot so that at the end of the last row (thirtieth from the beginning) you will have five meshes, the same number as at the starting end. As the mesh size is 2" stretched measure, the 30 rows will give a length of 60" to the net when stretched. Hang it on ¼ basis which means 16 inches stretched netting to the foot of hung netting. Thus 60 inches of stretched netting hangs as 45 inches.

Take a heavy cord 126 inches long similar to a heavy trot line or 84 thread cotton cord and tie the ends together thus making a loop 63 inches long. Of the 63 inches, 45 inches will have netting attached thus leaving nine inches on each end to be "whipped" to make the end rings or grommets.

CLAMP-ON LIVE BAG
*Note: Raw Edges Are Store Netting
—Yours Will Be Smooth*

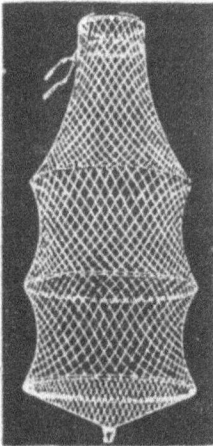

RING TYPE LIVE NET
*Readily Made On a
Netcraft Wheel*

Make This
Clamp-On Live Bag

THE CLAMP-ON frame shown here and available at Netcraft without the "store" netting, is 10 inches in diameter and has a circumference of 32 inches. Using a 1" square measure mesh and No. 12 twine there should be 28 starting meshes and the net should be from 30 to 42 inches deep or 15 to 21 meshes. Watch the job as it progresses and suit yourself as to depth.

Make the net full without any taper until you have the desired depth, then reduce two meshes each row until you have 22 loops left in a row. Seam up the sides if the work has been done in the flat—see page 14—then close the botton 22 meshes on a bone ring by the method shown on page 18.

The frame itself comes apart and permits you to thread the ring in and out of the top of the net until all meshes are on the frame.

IMPORTANT NOTE: An excellent net for this frame can be made with one yard (stretched measure) of three-foot wide netting ½" square mesh now available at Netcraft. Simply seam the side and close the bottom on a ring, then attach to the frame.

The ring type live net at left requires 10" to 14" rings. Use 1½" stretched measure mesh and sardine shuttle, No. 9 twine. Ten-inch requires 31 starting loops on wheel, and the 14" ring needs 40 starting meshes. Make the net about 26 meshes deep or to suit your own desires. Close the bottom on a bone ring and thread a piece of No. 60 twine for the top pucker string.

How To Make a Portable Live Box

HERE IS something almost every fisherman can profitably use. It is a live net made with 21" rings—big enough to let your fish swim and freely move about. Instead of keeping fish in shore live boxes which become warm and are subject to the abuse of sun, waves, and silt, try them in a live net weighted with a rock and let down in four to eight feet of water. There its colder, the water quiet and more nearly approximates their natural conditions.

There are two ways of making this net. One is to use factory made netting—1/2" square measure mesh; the other is to make the netting yourself using 3/4" square measure mesh.

Using factory made 1/2" square measure netting you'll need a piece 90 meshes around by 52 meshes deep. This can be procured by buying material that hangs three feet deep (which is approximately 52 meshes) and ask for 2 1/2 yards of it to get your 90 meshes around (stretched measure).

Bring the edges together on the three-foot side and seam up the net into a cylinder. This can be done by the method described on page 14 but a quick and easy way to do it is to bring the edges over a single nail. Now simply lace the seam closed and about every third mesh tie a half hitch. Keep plenty of tension on the net and the lacing string. When you get to the last mesh tie it twice so that it won't slip.

Now lace a bottom pucker string in and out of every bottom mesh and pull tight and tie.

Insert a 21" ring. Stretch tightly and twist the excess material so as to pull the material over the ring like a drum head. Using half a dozen little tie strings, tie the stretched netting to the bottom ring.

Now drop into the bag thus created two additional 2" rings. Lace another pucker string through all the top meshes and hang the affair on an overhead nail. Count about 10 meshes up from the bottom and tie one of the rings that you left in the bag in about half a dozen places around the net. Measure up about the same distance from the middle ring and tie the top ring in place with little tie strings. After you have the net nicely balanced and the rings all secured in place you can do a professional job by tying a series of half hitches all the way around each ring with one continuous string as shown on Page 29.

In the second method wherein you make the netting, use a gage to give you a 1½" stretched measure mesh, or ¾" square measure, and a Sardine shuttle and No. 9 twine. Make a piece of netting 60 meshes around by 36 meshes deep. This can be done in the flat by having 36 starting meshes on your rod, then knit 60 meshes deep. If a netting wheel is used the first three rows of knots should be 40 meshes, then increase five meshes each row with a plain row in between until the web has 60 meshes around. Now continue the knitting until the web is 36 meshes deep. The 40-mesh end of the cylinder should be the top of the net.

After the web is finished close the bottom with a pucker string and do all other operations just as described in attaching a factory made piece of netting.

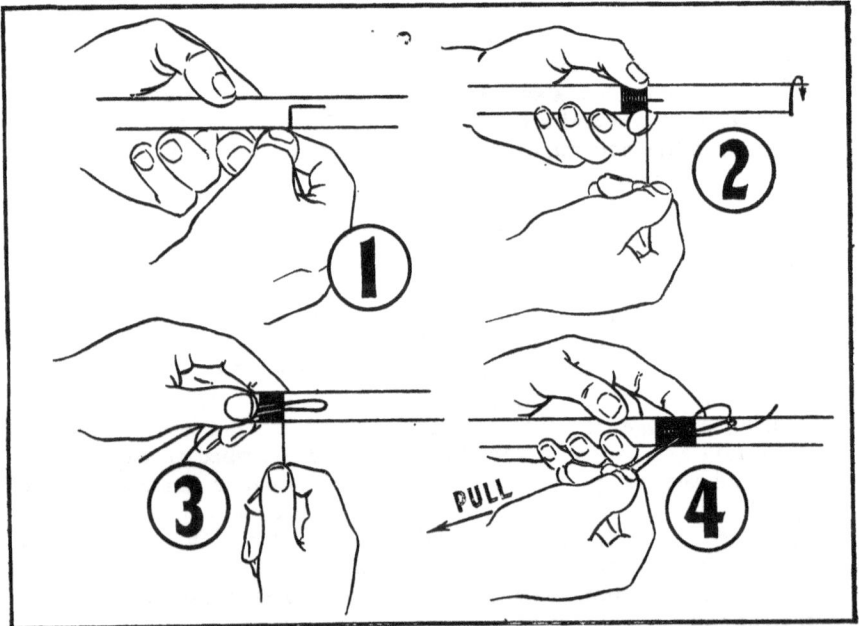

LEARN THIS HANDY WHIPPING TRICK. Here is something every fisherman should know: whipping with cord or twine. Use it rewrapping rods, whipping down the guides, making slip proof handles by whipping with seine twine and finishing with varnish or shellac. You'll find your shuttle a handy way to hold the twine or thread while winding. The whole trick is at the end to simply lay a separate loop of twine across your work, make three loose turns over this loop, tuck the loose end through the loop and pull out.

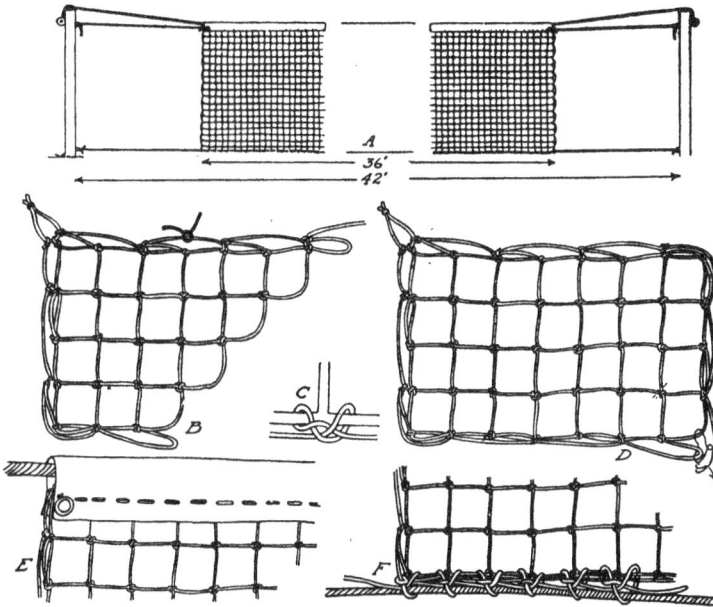

HOW TO MAKE A TENNIS NET

Fascinating Fun!

THE DIMENSIONS of a net to fit a standard size court in terms of the netting unit or mesh (1½" square) is 280 meshes long by 20 meshes wide.

This net is suspended by ropes between posts spaced 42 feet apart. The posts are 3'6" above ground and the top rope may be carried over the top of each post. Sufficient tension is placed on the rope to raise the middle point of the net three feet above the ground. A hold down loop of canvas not to exceed 12" in width may be used to control this height.

Start the netting on a foundation loop as indicated in Sketch B shown in the upper left hand corner. The completed rectangle is shown in Sketch D which also shows the method of closing the last mesh, lower right hand corner of Sketch D. The net is attached to the suspension ropes as indicated in Sketch F, using a cord and the seizing knot (Miller's Sack Knot) shown in Sketch C. The upper edge is covered with a piece of canvas as indicated by Sketch E, either machine or hand stitched.

The netting needle, mesh stick and foundation loop are shown in Sketch 1. Net two loops on the foundation loop, see Sketch 4, as indicated by Sketches 2 and 3. Sketch 5 shows the foundation loop turned over. Continue netting as indicated by Sketches 6 and 7. Sketch 8 shows how

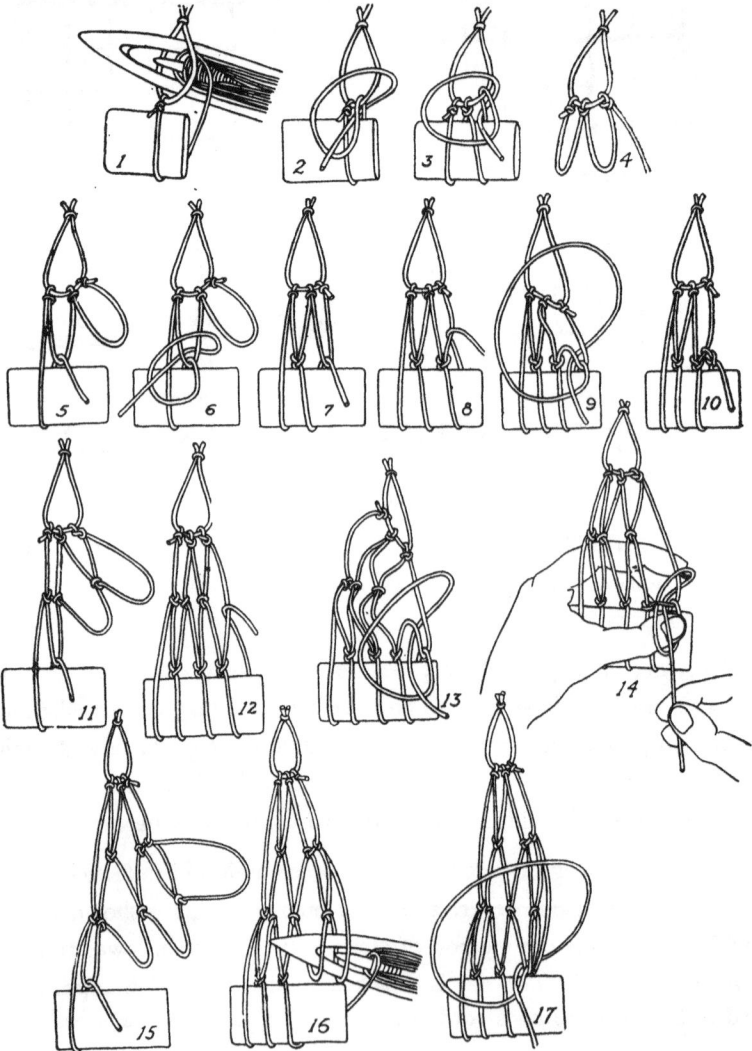

additional loops may be formed by going through the same loop twice. Sketches 9 and 10 indicate the process known as increasing. Turn the foundation loop over, see Sketch 11, and continue netting as shown by Sketches 12 and 13. Sketch 14 shows the manipulation in forming the knot on top of the mesh stick.

Continue this process until a 20-mesh width is obtained. Maintain width by keeping the number of meshes equal in each row by DECREAS-ING THE LENGTH ONE MESH (by netting the last two loops together) as indicated in Sketches 16 and 17. On the next row increase by one mesh as shown in Sketches 13 and 14. Repeat and alternate this procedure. Continue this process for 280 meshes, then decrease at the end of each row to fill out the corner. See Sketches B and D. This completes the net with a single cord fabric.

To make a net with the center section reinforced proceed as follows: Net a rectangular area 93 meshes long by 20 meshes wide and complete the corner as described above. Reload the netting needle with twine from two balls and net a rectangular area 94 meshes long and 20 meshes wide. Complete the corner by decreasing one mesh at the end of each row. Reload the netting needle with a single twine and net another rectangular area 93 meshes long and 20 meshes wide. Finish out corner. Attach the net to the suspension ropes as indicated in Sketches E and F.

Material: 4 balls No. 21 Seine Twine for single net (5 balls for reinforced center); one piece of canvas 4" wide, 36" long; 90 feet of ⅜" rope, 10 feet of ¼" rope.

How To Make a Fancy Hammock Attachment To Ring

(Continued From Page 28)

and tie it temporarily at the nail. Th s extra cord will serve to make the outside rigging line a double line instead of a single line.

Now contnue with the next row, using the cord at the furtherest right as the threading cord and weave it exactly as explained above and pass the leftmost cord through the same channel, tying both cords on the nail. Thus in each row you dispose of two cords, until you get to the last when there are only four cords left,.... take two of them in the left hand and two in the right and tie a simple knot to finish the job. The ends of these rigging lines are now passed through holes in the spreader stick for attaching to the previously finished net and braided lines.

BASKET-BALL NET DETAILS

USING the same method of net making as described for landing nets you can make a pair of basket-ball nets which will be every bit as professional in appearance as the ones sold in sporting goods stores. Before attempting the net, however, it is recommended that you practice making netting with any odd pieces of twine. See page 16 for details of the netting knot.

BASKET-BALL NET SPECIFICATIONS:

Twine Size: For school nets getting hard use an 84-thread twine (approximately 1/8" diameter) is used. This size, however, can be smaller to suit the material at hand. Anything smaller than No. 36 is apt to wear out too quickly.

Mesh Size: 5½" stretched measure.

Number of Meshes: 14 meshes, around the net. Seven meshes deep.

The completed net ready to hang measures 30 inches long at the top if stretched tight (it is doubled, of course). Now at the bottom the net measures 26¼ inches, thus making it slightly drawn in effect. This is accomplished by cutting a gage stick measuring only five inches around to make a 5-inch stretched measure mesh instead of 5½" as used at the top. This smaller gage is used only on the last row of meshes. When made of 84 thread cotton twine, the completed net weighs six ounces.

The finished net is fastened to the basket-ball goal or hoop by a series of half hitches. Space the meshes equally around the hoop. Coaches frequently use a little adhesive tape to hold the net securely in place.

HOW TO MEND NETS

Valuable Information For Every Sportsman
and Commercial Fisherman

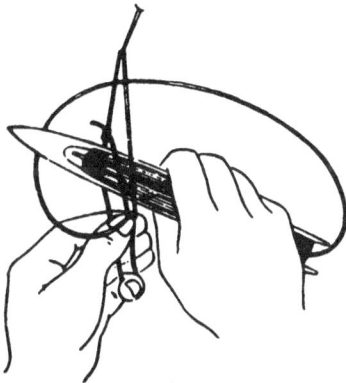

(A) *Making the knot.*

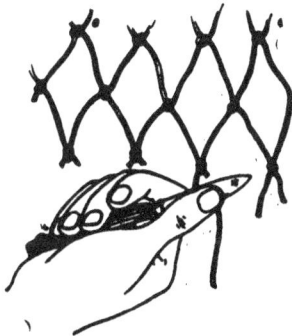

(B) *Cutting twine.*

HERE are a few tricks of the trade that are well worth having in handy reference form so that when the occasion arises you may mend a torn net or replace a whole section as the need may require. The commercial fisherman, of course, will find it of practical value to acquire this skill and even make a point of practicing various kinds of repair.

In all mending the gage stick is not used, as the twine is held between the fingers as shown in Figure (A). To become thoroughly proficient in mending one should also learn the trick of working from right to left (the customary gage stick method you will recall is always left to right). Follow the pictures at the end of this section and with a few practice meshes, you'll have it.

Notice the illustration titled "A Tear Before Trimming"—this shows a vertical and a horizontal tear. The first step in mending a tear is to cut off unnecessary tag ends, then cut enough more strands to satisfy the following requirements. (The second picture in this series shows the most convenient method of cutting twine.)

1. The end of the twine must start at a knot joining THREE strands or from a tag end leading from such a knot. The weaving must also end at a similar point. This is necessary because only one end of the mending twine is attached at the knots

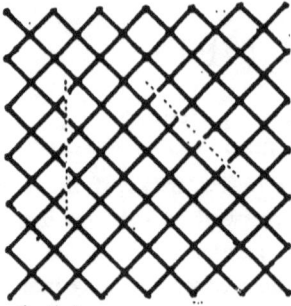

(C) Tear before trimming.

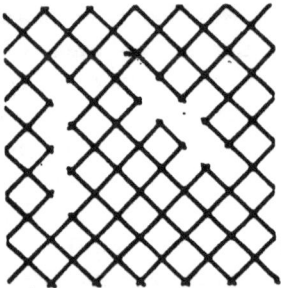

(D) Tear after trimming.

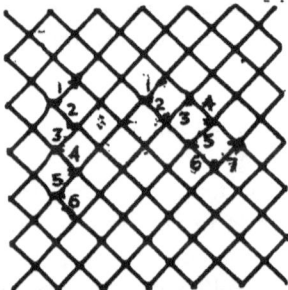

(E) Sequence of mending.

and there must be three unbroken strands of the original net to give the required four strands radiating from each knot.

2. The knots around the edges of the tear must have TWO unbroken strands of the original net. Figures C, D, and E show different typical tears before and after trimming, and the sequence in which the tears are woven.

If the mending starts at a knot where three strands join, the end of the twine should be tied on as shown in Figures F and G.

The end of the twine is placed between two of the strands, and the first hitch is made around these two strands. The second hitch is made around the middle strand only, in order to bind the end of the twine more securely without excessively distorting the shape of the mesh. If the mending starts at a tag end, the end of the twine is tied to the tag end with a square knot.

Similar ties are used in finishing the repair. The sequence of weaving depends upon the shape and position of the tear with respect to the weave of the net and must be determined for each job. See Figure (E) which shows by numbers the sequence or order in which the knots were tied. For beginners the most convenient method for finding the proper sequence

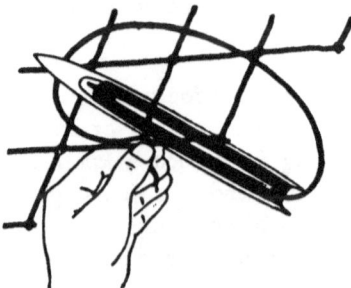

(F) First hitch in repair.

(G) Second hitch.

and weaving the tear is to spread the net out flat so that the meshes are square and thread the twine through the meshes (without tying it at the knots) until the proper sequence is found by trial. The twine may then be cut and left in the net to guide the weaving. The guiding twine is removed after the repair is finished.

In adjusting a loop, care must be taken to note whether the loop forms one or two sides of a mesh and to adjust the size accordingly.

On some complicated tears it is impossible to trim the tear so that it may be woven in a continuous sequence, without cutting out an excessive amount of the net. In such cases, it is better to trim less extensively and weave several sequences.

PATCHING.   When a net contains a large hole it is best to insert a patch cut from a scrap net or to weave a patch separately and then insert it in the hole.

First lay the net out and pull the meshes square. Then cut the hole out to a roughly rectangular shape surrounded by knots joining two strands. See Figure 1. Notice that a "three stranded" knot is not used for starting or finishing the insertion of the patch. This is because the weaving starts and finishes at the same knot when inserting a patch rather than at different knots as in mending a tear.

A rectangular patch is now cut or woven with one less "two stranded knot" on each side than on the corresponding side of the hole. See Figure (J). The patch is inserted in the net by weaving continuously around as shown in Figure 20. The numbers beside each strand indicate the order in which they were tied.

(H) Completed hitch.

(I) Hole trimmed for patch

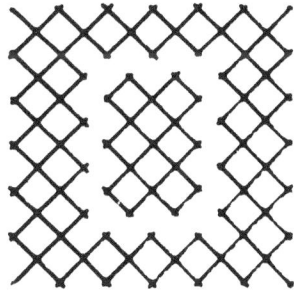

(J) Placing patch

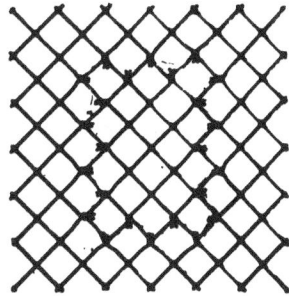

(K) Completed repair.

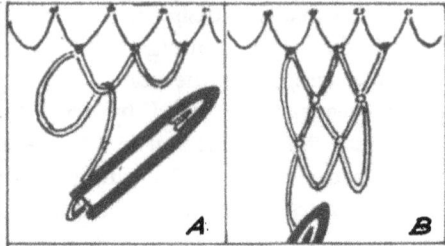

HOW TO MAKE A

SHOPPING BAG

●

H ERE IS a right handy shopping bag — folds up to a mere handful to slip into a purse or pocket yet holds a surprising amount. You'll like the nice comfortable feel of the handles—something really new and different.

Use No. 16 soft twine, knitting the net either flat on a rod or better yet, do it on a Netcraft Wheel. Use medium gage making approximately $2\frac{1}{2}$-inch stretched measure mesh. Make 36 starting meshes, then go straight down for 17 rows of knots. Then decrease four meshes in each of the following rows—18th, 20th, 22nd, the ones in between being regular without reductions. On the 24th reduce two mesh, then knit one row plain which should leave you with 22 meshes at the bottom and these you attach on a bone ring as shown on Page 18. If you are not using the Netcraft Wheel you should now close your net by the method shown in Fig. 166 on page 14.

At the top of the net bag do the cord finish Fig. H, Page 34. This gives you a ring to which the handles are attached. To make the handles, thread your shuttle with a double thread. Tie on to any mesh and using gage stick attach two meshes to the net as shown in the picture. Pull out gage stick, turn net over and do two more meshes. Continue this way, pulling out the gage stick for each row until you have created a handle eight rows of knots long. Now simply attach the final end of the handle to the net in the same way that you started the handle, to make it nine rows of knots long counting both attachments as a row. Leave five open meshes below each handle at the two ends and seven meshes on each side between the two handles. After making one bag you can change the size larger or smaller to suit your own personal preferences.

TYPES OF NETS — HOW USED
Tunnel or Hoop Net — No Wings

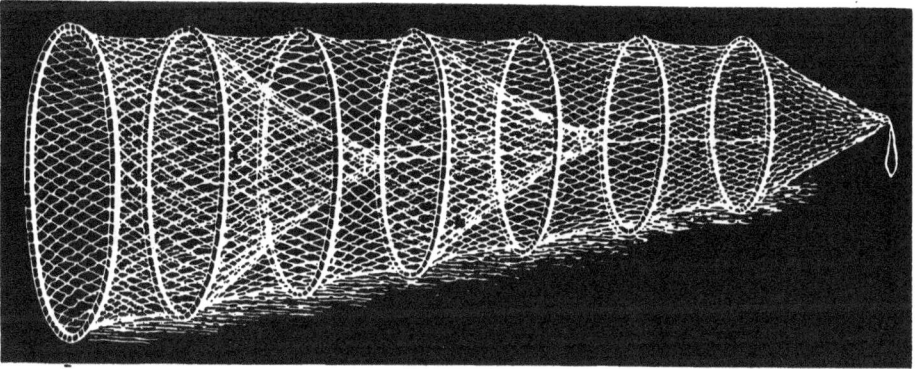

HOOP NETS are used as traps and are very effective in rivers and other waters where fish "run" in some general direction. The fish work through the throats or funnels and are unable to find their way out again. Bait is sometimes attached inside the nets to attract fish. Hoop nets are made up in sizes from two-foot diameter mouth openings to five-foot mouth opening, and in lengths from six feet for the smaller diameter to 18 feet for the five-foot diameter. The number of hoops vary from four to eight. When this net is made up with wings which are weighted and corked, it is known as a Fyke Net. The purpose of the wings is to "lead" the fish into the net.

Fyke Net With Wings

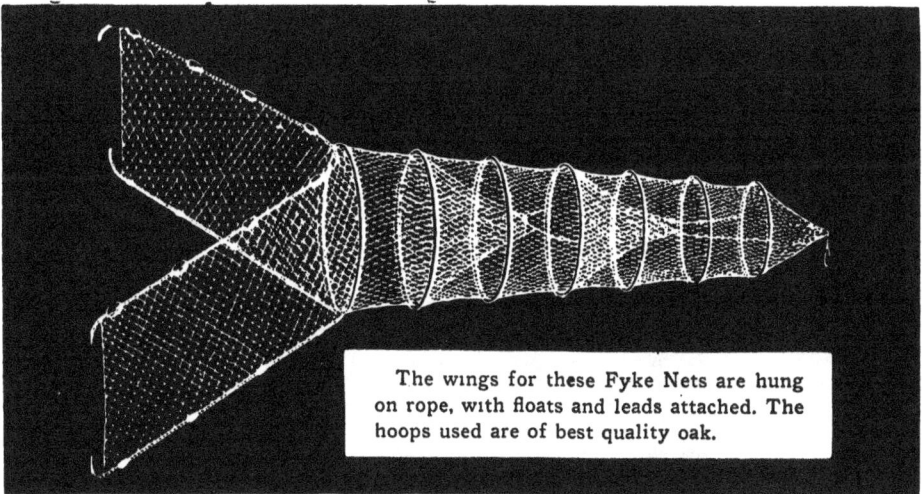

The wings for these Fyke Nets are hung on rope, with floats and leads attached. The hoops used are of best quality oak.

Types of Nets (Continued)
THE BROOK HOOP NET

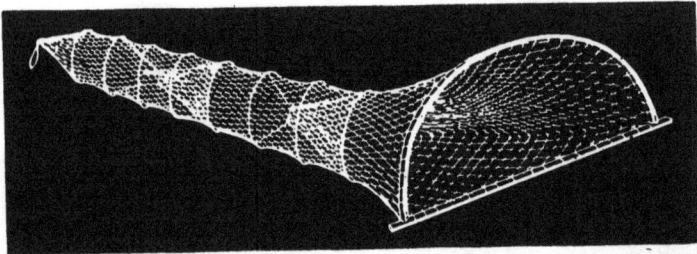

Obviously this net is just the thing for smaller fish and for bait. To get those nice big brook chubs which are "killers," as live bait, a net of this type will interest many sportsmen and bait dealers.

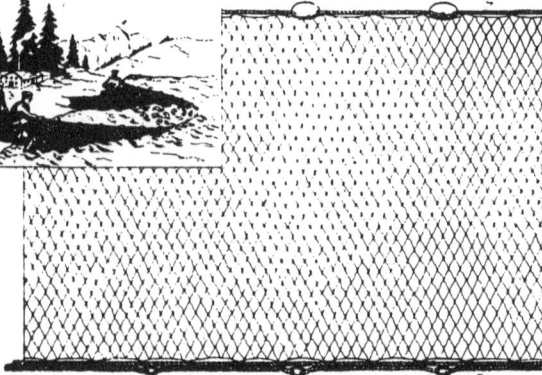

———●———

STRAIGHT AND TAPERED SEINES

This is probably the oldest type of fish net which is known. In its simplest form it may be a little one man minnow net pushed ahead of the fisherman with a pair of stakes. In its commercial form it may be hundreds of yards long requiring a powerful ship—a "dragger"—to encircle the school. Both straight and tapered seines as here illustrated are usually hung in one-third basis, which means using 18 inches of netting (stretched) to 12 inches of rope. The top line is single and the bottom line is double of opposite twist or lay to prevent the seine from rolling. Straight seines are ordered by the fisherman to suit his own ideas and he specifies the depth in number of meshes, size of mesh, and basis or fullness in hanging. Straight seines are most generally made up in soft laid twine.

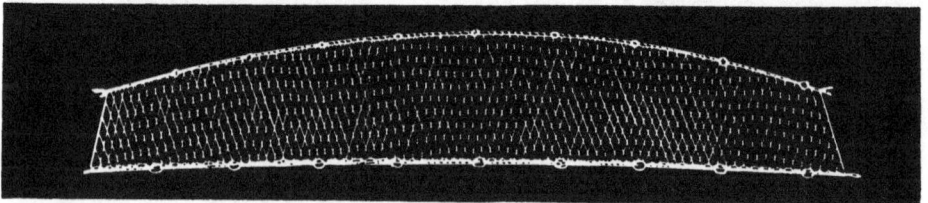

Types of Nets (Continued)
GILL OR SET NET

An interesting kind of net is the gill net, drift net, or set net as it is sometimes called. It is like a seine, except that it is not used to enclose schools of fish. It is set out by means of weights and floats, like a wall of net. The fish try to get through the meshes of the net but only their heads will go through. The meshes are too small for their bodies. They try to back out and their gills are caught in the net. Gill nets are usually set on the bottom and stretched out as taut as possible by means of some kind of anchorage. They are made of strong fine thread, usually linen.

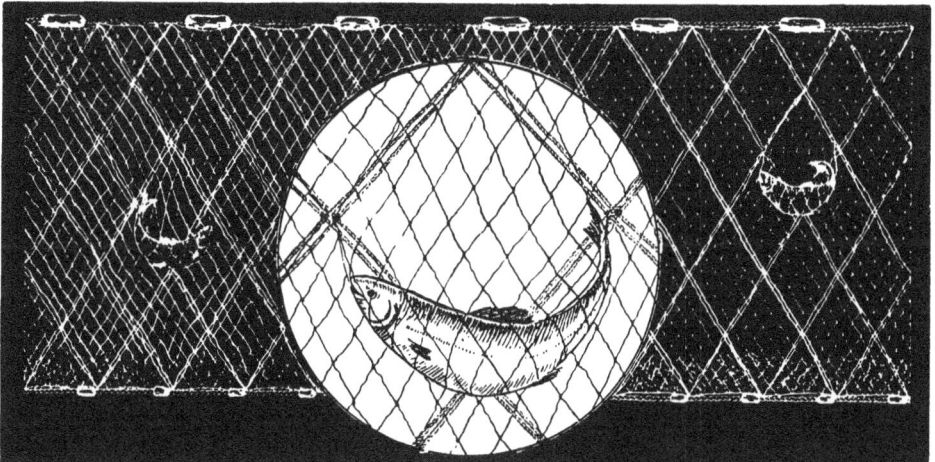

TRAMMEL NETS Trammel Nets are made up of three sheets of netting: one web of small mesh usually of linen twine is hung between two outer webs or "walls" of large mesh cotton. The net is set taut across a stream, and fish striking it push the fine inside netting through the larger meshes of the "walls" and thus pocket themselves.

Types of Nets (Continued)

POUND NET — SHORT TUNNEL

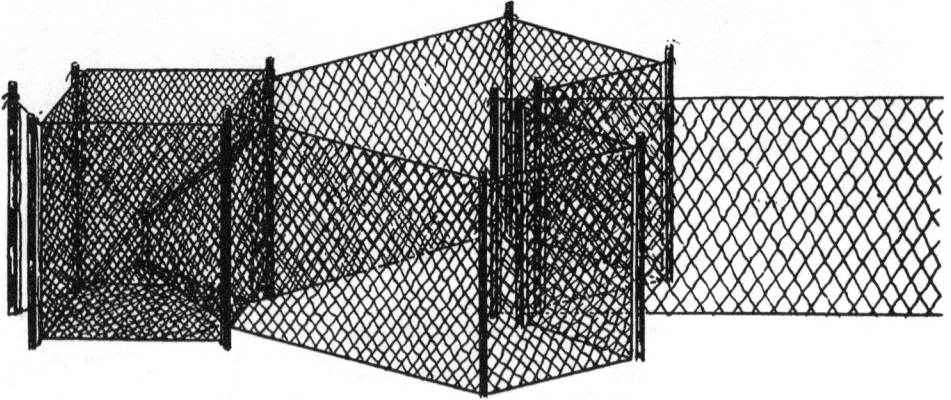

This is the pound net, or Weir net so widely used and familiar to commercial fishermen everywhere. Note: The word pound comes from an old Anglo-Saxon word meaning an inclosure. Our dog pound comes from the same word.

Essentially the operation of the pound net is similar to the Lake Erie Trap, except that the leaders. etc., are supported on stakes. It is generally agreed that the construction of the tunnel is the most important part in building these nets. It must be just right so the fish will find their way easily into the Pot, without loose flopping web to scare them back or dark spots to seem like obstructions. The great majority of Pound Nets are constructed with the web hung on "1/3 basis."

HELPFUL TABLES OF NETTING WEIGHTS

Cotton Netting

SQUARE FEET IN ONE POUND — ON 1/3 BASIS

Mesh	1"	1⅛"	1¼"	1½"	2"	2¼"	3"	4"
6 Thd	37	45	49	64	90	115	142	194
9 "	22		32	40	58	72	90	130
12 "	15		22	28	40	53	68	95
15 "	9		14	22	31	43	52	72
18 "				16	25	34	42	58
21 "					21	29	36	49
24 "		8¼	8½	13	19	25	29	40
27 "					13½	20	26	35
30 "					12½	18	22	32
36 "					10	14	19	28
42 "						10	16	22
48 "							13	21
54 "							11¼	16½
60 "							10½	15
72 "							8	

Linen Netting To Hang 50' Long

25/3 CORD

Feet Deep	Size Mesh Square	Pounds	Feet Deep	Size Mesh Square	Pounds
3	1¾	1/4	5	2½	3/8
	2	1/4		3	1/4
	2½	1/5			
			6	1¼	3/4
4	1	3/4		1½	3/4
	1½	2/5		1¾	1/2
	1¾	2/5		2	1/2
	2	3/8		2½	3/8
	2½	1/4		3	3/8
5	1¼	3/4	8	1½	7/8
	1½	1/2		1¾	3/4
	1¾	1/2		2	3/4
	2	7/16		2½	1/2
				3	2/5

HINTS ON PRESERVING NETS

THE PROBLEM of preserving nets is a serious one for the commercial fisherman. Volumes have been written on the subject and research is constantly going on endeavoring to find better methods. It is said that for each dollar American fishermen receive for their catch, 20c is paid out for nets.

Space here does not permit a detailed account of all preservative methods. However, a book on net making would not be complete without touching upon the various methods used and emphasizing some hints of netting care applicable to the sport fisherman.

The heavy nets used in pound nets, traps, heavy seines, etc., are dipped in hot tar. Frequently, before tarring, the net is given a chemical treatment which keeps down the bacterial action that tends to digest the cotton.

Light nets, such as gill netting and all nets not tarred, are treated in various ways. Nets freshly contaminated with slime are rinsed with lime water. Lime water is easily prepared by keeping a few inches of slaked lime in a barrel and adding as much fresh or salt water as possible, with stirring. After the milky color disappears the solution is ready for use.

DIRECT SUNSHINE RUINS NETS. ALL NETS SHOULD BE DRIED AND STORED WHERE THE SUN WILL NOT SHINE ON THEM. Many tests have proved beyond question that sunshine is extremely harmful to nets. One gill netter saved himself $2.00 each summer fishing day by drying his nets in the shade.

A recent development in the commercial fishing industry is Liquid Copper. This is highly effective in killing the bacteria that ruin nets, furthermore, it has the advantage of leaving the net soft and pliable. Numerous tests have proved its effectiveness and accordingly it is the one kind of preservative recommended by Netcraft. Requires no heating or cooking. Mixes with gasoline or kerosene. Nets are simply dipped in it and hung up to drain.

In conclusion, here are some simple rules to follow: Keep your net clean. Wash off all slime as soon as possible. Avoid sunshine. Keep nets from alternately soaking and drying in the usually fouled water in the bottom of a fishing boat. A good and inexpensive preservative, used by menhadden fishermen, is to dip the net in strong salt brine and let dry. This "pickles" the net.

BIG NETS IN ACTION

"I must go down to the seas again, for the call of the running tide
Is a wild call and a clear call that may not be denied."

—JOHN MASEFIELD

MOST OF us land-bound sport fishermen have a touch of the "Sea Fever" that sends men off to the vagrant gypsy life, where the white clouds are flying, the sea-gull's crying, and the wind's like a whetted knife. Not only do our fancies often turn to the sea but to the men who wrest their living from it and the nets and gear they use. It is appropriate, therefore, that we include in this manual on Net Making a little about some of our present day fishing methods where the Big Nets go in action.

TRAWLERS.   Under Diesel power, boats like the one pictured above, drag large, bag-shaped nets about 150 feet long over the sea bed. The bag, called a Cod End, is kept open by the pressure of the sea against two large wooden frames called "Doors" which are attached by ropes or chains ahead of the Cod End. The average drag is an hour and fifteen minutes at about 11 knots. The net is hoisted over the deck by a powerful winch and the Cod End opened, dropping the fish to the deck.

For the next hour and a quarter the crew sort and gut the catch, until time for the next haul to be made. In the modern trawler there are two trawl nets, one on the port and one on the starboard side. Repairs to nets are made between hauls. Dragging goes on day and night. Cod, haddock, soles and flounders are taken by this method, commonly called Otter **Trawling.**

BIG NETS IN ACTION—Purse Seining

Here is a gull's eye view of a trip you are about to take aboard a Mackerel Seiner. The pages that follow show the big seine in action.

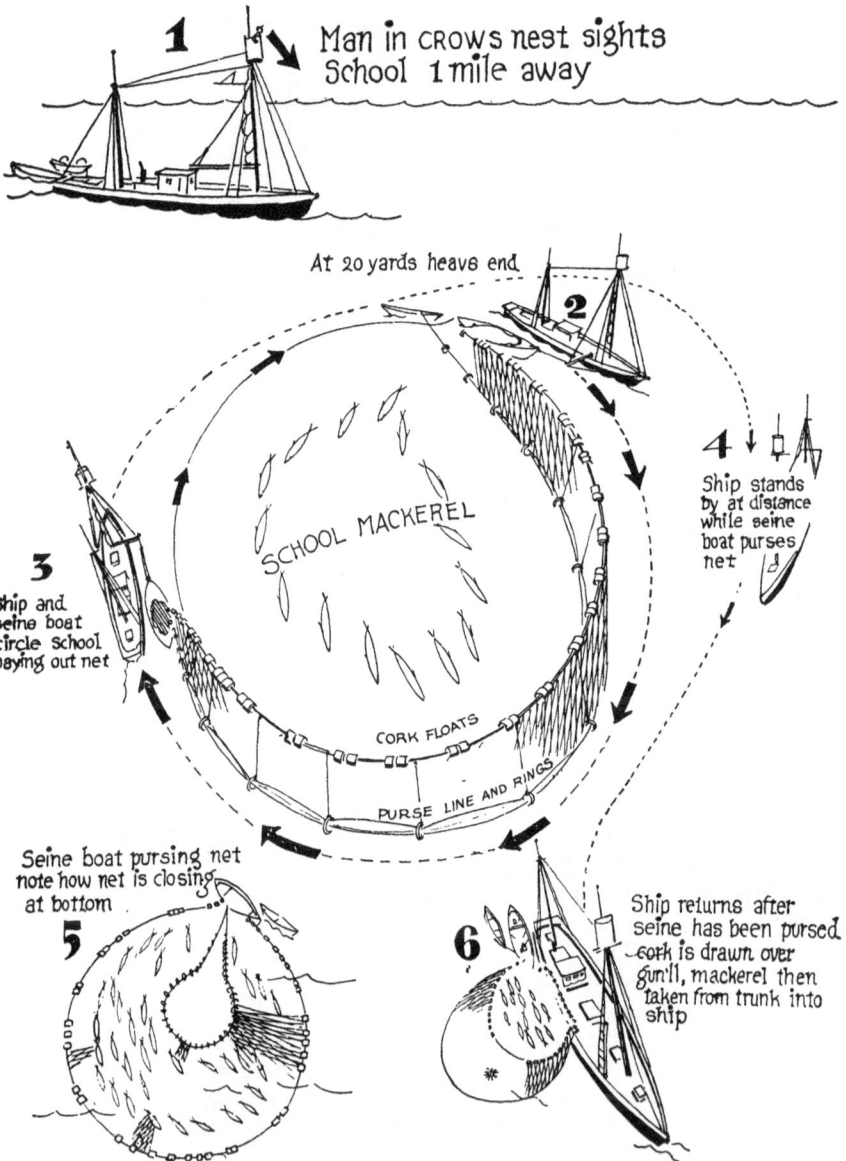

1 Man in CROWS nest sights School 1 mile away

At 20 yards heave end

2

4 Ship stands by at distance while seine boat purses net

3 Ship and seine boat circle school paying out net

SCHOOL MACKEREL

CORK FLOATS

PURSE LINE AND RINGS

Seine boat pursing net note how net is closing at bottom

5

6 Ship returns after seine has been pursed cork is drawn over gun'll, mackerel then taken from trunk into ship

Pictorial Trip Aboard a Mackerel Seiner

In this method of fishing the school of fish, usually mackerel, are sighted by a lookout up in the crow's nest and the fish are then encircled while the seine is paid out from a seine boat which in turn is being towed by the big Seiner. Above you see the start of encircling the school and below you see the closing of the big circle. (Continued on next page.)

PICTORIAL TRIP ABOARD A PURSE SEINER (Continued)

Upper Left—The big net is being pursed together thus making a bottom to the big "sack" which encircles the fish.

Upper Right—The seine has now been narrowed to a small circle only a few yards across.

Below, Upper Left—The big seiner now draws alongside and the pursed seine, now actually boiling with fish, is emptied by the power operated dip net shown on the right.

Lower Views, Left to Right—Time out for a well earned lunch. *Middle View*—The Purse Seiner and seine boat.

Notice the crow's nest. *Right*—The seine boat and crew now clear all their gear and prepare for further action.

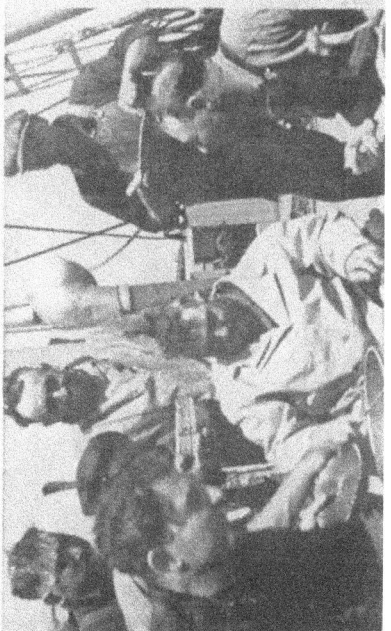

PICTORIAL TRIP ABOARD A PURSE SEINER (Continued)

Here we see the harvest—a thrilling sight as thousands of pounds of Mackerel fresh from the sea are dumped aboard the big seiner.

BIG NETS IN ACTION (Gill Netting)

The method by which fish are caught in gill nets is illustrated on page 57. In brief, the fish try to get through the meshes but only their heads will go through. They try to back out and their gills are caught in the net. Here we see one of a fleet of big Atlantic gill netters. Notice the gill net, loaded with fish, being brought over the side between rollers.

A Modern Gill Netter Fishing Out of Gloucester

BIG NETS IN ACTION (Gill Netting, Continued)

GILL NETTING is carried on in fishing waters throughout the globe and involving equipment and fishing craft from scarcely no larger than a row boat all the way to the big Atlantic boats shown on the previous page.

Gill Netting, for example, off southern Long Island, New York, is done with smaller boats and smaller gill nets than done by the gill netters off Gloucester. Lake Michigan, and other Great Lakes gill fishermen bring in a sizable portion of the total fish landings. The hazards are often great, the expensive gill nets being sometimes a complete loss after a violent lake storm.

The pictures here tell their own story. You see the big gill net, with floats attached being paid out over the stern. After all the net is out an anchor buoy is made fast which both marks the net and anchors it taut for proper fishing. The beau-

BIG NETS IN ACTION (Gill Netting, Continued)

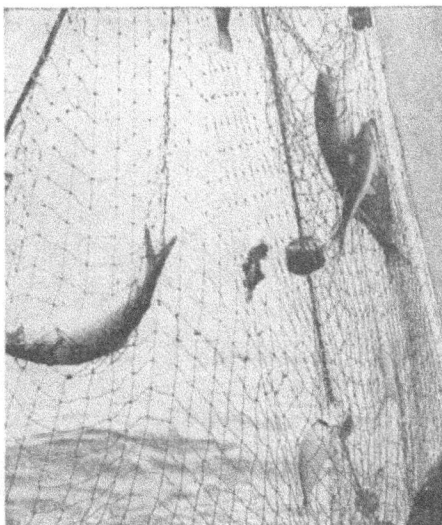

tiful fish, caught in the meshes, often in unbelievable numbers, all appear about the same size, the smaller ones, of course, passing right on through the net.

If you are observing you will notice that the fisherman holding the gill net in the upper left view has some mending to do—part of the everyday chores of the commercial fisherman. Below you see the big reels for drying the netting.

RELAX AND ENJOY YOURSELF

THE FISHERMAN'S sport is unique indeed. He enjoys not only the highest adventure out in the open on streams and lakes, but throughout the year there is rare pleasure in keeping up the tackle and planning for the fun ahead.

As in Net Making, there are other unique side adventures you can now explore. For example, touch up all your bass plugs, spinners, floats, etc., with Netcraft Lacquer Kit,—even make your own baits, it's great fun. Or, take that tackle box and fix it up with cork lining throughout,—the Netcraft Cork Kit contains everything you'll need. And for completely working over your tackle the Netcraft Tackle Saver Kit will provide hours of profitable enjoyment.

Leathercloth, now available by the yard, offers much pleasure in making rod cases, boat cushions, doing home upholstery work. And in this connection you must learn the trick of using the Sportsmen's Hand Stitcher that sews the lock stitch.

Still another "do-it-yourself" adventure is smoking and curing fish at home or camp. Curing fish has long been the guarded secret of a few. Now with Netcraft's profusely illustrated book you can get set to enjoy one of the swellest food treats imaginable. Here is another fine "picture book" for the fellow who cares to leave the conventional paths in seeking fishin' fun.

We believe you'll be well repaid by carefully reading Netcraft's catalog of hard to find specialties for fishermen. Needless to say, you'll find listed there all the needed supplies for netmaking.

No matter what may be your daily grind, a little time out to relax and "tinker," like our friend in the picture on the opposite page, pays great dividends. Here's wishin' you new adventure and the best of fishin' fun.

H. T. LUDGATE
Netcraft Co.

TO TIE LINE TO LEADER

12 *Jam Hitch with Knot*

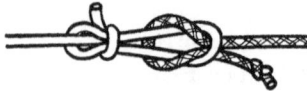

13 *Pinch Jam*

14 *Tiller Hitch*

15 *Figure Eight*

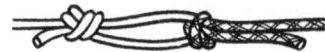

16 *Jam Knot*

17 *Jam Hitch*

ATTACHING LEADER TO EYED FLIES OR HOOKS

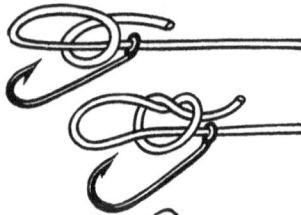

18 *Turle Knot*

19 *Half Hitch Jam*

20 *Eyed Fly Jam*

21 *Wemyss Eyed Fly Knot*

22 *Jam Double Hitch*

23 *Wedge*

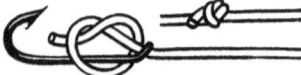

24 *Jam Hitch with Knot*